T0193834

SEMIOTEXT(E) INTERVENTION SERIES

© 2010 by Gerald Raunig

Published by Semiotext(e)
PO Box 629, South Pasadena, CA 91031
www.semiotexte.com

Design: Hedi El Kholti
Inside cover photographs: Cheryl Dunn

ISBN: 978-1-58435-085-9
Distributed by The MIT Press, Cambridge, Mass.
and London, England

Gerald Raunig

A Thousand Machines

A Concise Philosophy of the Machine
as Social Movement

Translated by Aileen Derieg

semiotext(e)
intervention
series □ 5

Contents

1

BICYCLES

If you let it go too far it would be the end of everything.
You would have bicycles wanting votes and they would
get seats on the County Council and make the roads far
worse than they are for their own ulterior motivation.
But against that and on the other hand, a good bicycle is
a great companion, there is a great charm about it.
— Flann O'Brien, *The Third Policeman*

"Is it about a bicycle?" This is the central question of the two policemen in Flann O'Brien's novel *The Third Policeman*. In this novel the representatives of the state apparatus mainly have to deal with bicycles, with the theft of bicycles or of bicycle bells, air pumps, dynamos and lights. Horns, rims, saddles, racing pedals, three-speed gearshifts, cycle clips and similar extras are the components of a refined and extensive discourse, from which there is no escape. Police virtuosity even extends all the way to stealing bicycles themselves, in order to solve the crime. They are all the more annoyed when the answer to the question is no.

If it *is* about a bicycle, however, the matter comes into full bloom. At first the bicycle appears to be quite a simple technical machine. With some interest and some insights into the science of mechanics, a person could easily grasp how it works. In his novel, however, written in 1940 and published in 1967, Flann O'Brien sketches an overwhelmingly fluid relationship between the bicycle and the human being. In the parish of the *Third Policeman* atomic theory is at work, a strange theory that deals with the mutual exchange, the flowing of atoms, the particles of matter; and this means not only the flowing *within* precisely delimited bodies and identities, but rather the unbounded flow *between* bodies that touch or come close to one another, that merge into one another in neighboring zones. This flowing is found, for instance, between the feet of a walker and the open road, between the horse and its rider, between the smith's hammer and an iron bar. Conjunctions, connections, couplings, transitions, concatenations.

The astonishing point of this elaborate invention: the more time a person spends on their bicycle, the more their personality mingles with the personality of the bicycle. This has specific consequences, especially for the modes of movement and the phenomena accompanying them: humans who always move along walls, walk as continuously as possible, never sit down, and prop themselves up with their arms and lean against a wall when they stop, completely shifting their weight to the tip of an elbow or propping themselves up with one foot on the curb. In the worst case, if they move too slowly or stop in the middle of the street, they fall face forward and have to be helped up or pushed along. Consequently, in *The Third Policeman* there are more or less precise calculations in relation to the question of to which percent this composite and moving assemblage, this machine, is now a bicycle and to which percent it is a human being—this percentage calculation is naturally worst for the postman. It appears, however, that the guardians of law and order charged with this matter never quite get their task under control, never illuminate the whole picture, are never able to bring the flowing machinery entirely into the comprehensive spotlight of administration; and indeed there are bicycles with a high human portion, which obviously develop emotionality and sexuality, and occasionally food inexplicably disappears when they are near.

In Claude Faraldo's film *Themroc* (1972), orgiastically fleeing in all directions, there is a small scene, in which the machine human/bicycle falls over for a completely different reason: not because its human portion is vanishing, but because a complementary social component that it depends on is withdrawn. Social dependency and subjection permeate the first part of the film, which starts with a representation of the stereotype of a fordist working day. Even life outside work, getting ready to go to work every morning and the way to work, correspond to the logic of the conveyor belt: the factory, the job, the way there are divided up into small portions in a time grid and standardized. Even before breakfast the recurrent perspective of the kitchen clock, both a technical and a social machine, follows the striated time of the factory. Deviance only develops in the absolute interior of the isolated private imagination, such as the desire for his young sister, with whom the main figure Themroc, played by Michel Piccoli, still lives in their mother's small flat.

In the second scene the protagonist turns into the street with his bicycle from the back courtyard of his dilapidated housing estate. He does not merge haphazardly and randomly into the traffic then. As a fixed part of his way to work, exactly timed and made more precise through repetition, when he turns into the street he meets his colleague, who merges into the traffic with his bicycle at exactly the same moment from the opposite courtyard on the other side. Then both ride down the long straight street shoulder-on-shoulder, mutually supporting one another as *one* machine.

Sociality in fordism implies the simultaneity of social subjection and solidarity as mutual dependency. Masses streaming into the Metro, uniformity and repetition, the punch-clock, the omnipresent *dispositif* of discipline and surveillance that constitutes the subjects as cogs in the fordist social machine, inventing and interlocking many small machines at the same time. In *Themroc*, for instance, this is evident in the synchronicity of the anteroom supervisor's pencil sharpening machine and the secretary's manicure machine. And yet small differences flare up here and there. Themroc does not leave it at the omnipotence of the *dispositif*. The first larger outburst, the transformation in the toilet, the infectious roar, the turn to sexual liberation: what was already hinted at in the small deviant allusions at the beginning of the film proliferates in its course into a wild flight from the fordist constraints into an anarchic sphere.

Themroc is an agent of transition, the glimmering of a life that escapes the fordist regime. In this transition he invents new weapons. Instead of throwing a wooden shoe into the gears, his form of sabotage consists of fleeing from the factory. He flees, and in fleeing he changes the order of the factory changing room and that of public transportation by disrupting the schedule of the Metro by walking on the tracks. Power, power relations and power conditions prove to be ubiquitous, but Themroc's resistance is primal and productive. Fleeing from the setting of the factory, he invents an entirely new terrain. Interruptions, ruptures, refractions, fragmentations. In the midst of the fordist *dispositif* Piccoli draws a new *dispositif*, walling up the door to his room, tearing down the outside wall with a sledgehammer, tossing the furniture into the courtyard and beginning a wild new life.

The roaring, the smashing and the animalistic groaning—there is not a single word in a familiar language in the film—prove to be infectious. The attacks from the state apparatus seeking to reestablish order with manifold and yet simplistic means (persuasion, threats of the use of weapons, laughing gas, walling up) are repelled in laughter. In this setting, finally two of the policemen are roasted on a spit and eaten. And while Themroc/Piccoli attempts to live a different life inside his dwelling opened up to the outside and in new, free relationships, the next morning his colleague outside on the street experiences the withdrawal of the complementary social component: accustomed to the daily ritual of mutually supporting and being supported, as he turns into the street from the courtyard he overlooks the new situation—and abruptly falls over with his bicycle. This machine of social subjection, the synchrony of dependency and solidarity, no longer exists. The next morning the colleague has mounted training wheels on his bicycle.

In 1946 Luigi Bartolini published his novel *Ladri di Biciclette*. Shortly thereafter Vittorio de Sica transformed the material into a classic of Italian neo-realism, played by amateur actors, shot directly in the streets of Rome. *Bicycle Thieves* was released as a film in 1948. Bartolini had originally agreed to the filming, but then vehemently protested against de Sica's radical treatment. Although the script also varies the subject of the book in some places, the crucial turn from the book to the film emerges in the turn of the subject position: whereas the first-person narrator of the book, a bourgeois poet, who masterfully, distantly and moralizingly examines the psychology, philosophy and economy of the thieves of Rome as an autonomous artist-subject, the worker Antonio, protagonist of the neo-realist film, is "subject" in the contrary sense: he is *subjected* and exposed to the coercions of rough everyday life. For the hero of the book, the bicycle theft is his reason to begin a calm, planned, almost luxurious search; tracking down the bicycle or the thief and even the theft itself are staged as a gracious sport, even as art. For the anti-hero of the film, it is completely different: for him this turns into a manic, panicked movement, haphazard and driven, dependent on contingency and fortune-telling. Whereas the cycle of theft and re-aquisition in the anarchic geography of Rome moves the poet in the book to own two bicycles for security, Antonio, the protagonist in the film, is only able to keep his hands on his bicycle for a brief period of time: in the beginning of the film narration, in the midst of the unemployment and bitter poverty of the immediate post-war era, he gets a job hanging up posters, but only under the condition that he has a bicycle. His young family's bedsheets are brought to the pawn shop to redeem his old bicycle.

Antonio's bicycle is stolen on his very first day at work, while he is struggling on a ladder to hang up the first poster. It is not a solitary thief, but an assemblage of several components operating in a perfectly coordinated division of labor that first of all meticulously checks-out the territory. An inconspicuously dressed man casually places himself next to the bicycle, then another, younger man with a "German cap" waits for the right moment and quickly rides away with the bicycle. The first man pretends not to have noticed the theft and gets in Antonio's way seemingly accidentally, and finally a third man swings himself onto the car that Antonio has jumped onto for the chase and takes it in the wrong direction. Antonio doesn't stand a chance against this coordinated swarm of bicycle thieves. When he returns to the scene of the crime, all the possible witnesses have wandered off.

When Antonio attempts to win the police to recover his bicycle, a first policeman takes up the case, but then declines again immediately; the matter has been recorded, the victim should look for his bicycle himself. Even more so than the book, the film is devoted to the search for the bicycle that begins at this point, winding through the city from the black market at Piazza Vittorio to desperation at the Porta Portese, where the bicycle thieves return their loot into circulation in incredible amounts and a never-ending stream of newly pilfered material. If they think a bicycle will be too easily recognized, they take it apart, reducing it to all its single parts if necessary, and then they sell these individually—bells, brakes, saddles, pumps, pedals, dynamos, headlights, tires, etc. Antonio and his friends accordingly divide their attention, scanning the scenery: one looks at the frames, another at the tires, another at the bells and pumps. With the manifold strategies of disguise, however, such as switching single parts or repainting the bikes, the special characteristics of the bicycle are made to disappear, the identity of the bicycle can no longer be established. A second policeman quickly fetched to the scene does not appear to be particularly interested in solving the case either. In Bartolini's book there are even policemen among the peddlers at the black market, and the businesses of the official bicycle dealers are equally integrated in the network of bicycle thieves.

Alongside and below the both manic and unsuccessful search for the bicycle, the film also develops a study of the social machine of its thieves. At the Porta Portese Antonio suddenly sees the young thief who rode his bicycle away, but then he loses him again. When he discovers him a second time, he is able to pursue him and catch him in the street where his family lives. At the same time, he becomes acquainted with the social machine as an incomprehensible crowd. Half the neighborhood is in solidarity with the boy suffering an epileptic seizure, the policeman that is called in and searches the boy's flat persuades Antonio not to press charges. The social machine of the bicycle thieves becomes completely unbounded, its outlines diffuse, inside and outside no longer distinguishable. In consequence, in his desparation in the end, Antonio himself decides to become a bicycle thief—unsuccessfully, as he is caught at his first attempt.

The status of the worker-subject in the film, entirely subjected to economic conditions, sheds just as little light on the machinic setting of the bicycle thieves as the fictive sovereignty of the bourgeois poet-subject from the book. Even reading the very different fortunes of the protagonists in the narration from the original and from the film together does not really help us here. The two sides of the subject, which are so differently staged in the book and the film as either sovereign or subjected, this two-sided *dispositif* of social subjection is not sufficient to grasp the swarming machine of the bicycle thieves. Even a concept of the subject that dispenses with the dichotomy of sovereignty and subjection, even the complementary construction of the two poles only leads to a limited understanding of machinic modes of subjectivation. What is obviously involved here— in the swarm-shaped sociality of the bicycle thieves and the black markets—is a much more diffused form that does not first constitute subjects as a state apparatus through counting, measuring, striating, and then ensures their comprehensive social subjection and dependency. What seems to be at work here is an opaque form of *machinic enslavement* that is hard to grasp, inducing invention and cooperation without a visible hierarchy, without perceptible subjection, which is even capable of overcoding state apparatuses and feeding them into the dispositif of the machine.

The assemblage of the bicycle thieves also more clearly reveals the ambivalences of all three bicycle machines: the looming danger that bicycles would want to vote and claim a seat on the County Council, the integration of Themroc's rebellion—that is not shown in the film, but which we know has been accomplished since the 1970s—into difference capitalism, finally the machine of the bicycle thieves as mafiosi, perhaps even fascistoid micropolitics: these are the negative poles of a shimmering and alternating ambivalence of the machine. Yet against that and on the other hand, there is a great charm about it.

2

MACHINE FRAGMENTS

But, once adopted into the production process of capital, the means of labour passes through different metamorphoses, whose culmination is the machine, *or rather, an* automatic system of machinery *[…], set in motion by an automaton, a moving power that moves itself; this automaton consisting of numerous mechanical and intellectual organs, so that the workers themselves are cast merely as its conscious linkages.*
— Karl Marx, *Fragment on Machines*

On the contrary, we think that the machine must be grasped in an immediate relation to a social body and not at all to a human biological organism. Given this, it is no longer appropriate to judge the machine as a new segment that, with its starting point in the abstract human being in keeping with this development, follows the tool. For human being and tool are already machine parts on the full body of the respective society. The machine is initially a social machine, constituted by the machine-generating instance of a full body and by human being and tools, which are, to the extent that they are distributed on this body, machinized.
— Gilles Deleuze, Félix Guattari, *Anti-Oedipus*

Is it about a machine? The question is not easy to answer, but correctly posed. The question should certainly not be: What is a machine? Or even: Who is a machine? It is not a question of the essence, but of the event, not about *is*, but about *and*, about concatenations and connections, compositions and movements that constitute a machine. Therefore, it is not a matter of saying "the bicycle *is* …"—a machine, for instance, but rather the bicycle *and* the person riding it, the bicycle and the person *and* the bicycle and the person mutually supporting one another, the bicycles *and* the bicycle thieves, etc.

The commonplace concept of the machine, however, refers to a technical object, which can be precisely determined in its physical demarcation and seclusion, as well as in its usability for a purpose. Regardless of how these characteristics may be verified today, the machine was once conceptualized quite differently, namely as a complex composition and as an assemblage that specifically could not be grasped and defined through its utilization. The meaning of the term machine gradually began to be limited to its technical, mechanistic and seemingly clearly-delimitable sense starting in the 13th century and has been developed since the 17th century as a radical disambiguation of the term. The term entered into the German and the English languages through the influence of the French *machine* as a purely technical term alongside the still existent Latin *machina* concept and its derivatives. The enormous leap in the development of technical apparatuses and equipment in the 17th and 18th centuries, their dissemination and the knowledge about them in every possible field of society, was followed in the 19th century by the development of an economic *dispositif* of technical apparatuses, in other words a *dispositif* of the economic functionality and the exploitation of these apparatuses to increase productivity.

The vehement restraint of the broader concept of *machina* as an assemblage of concepts that was previously not at all only technically connotated thus first began in the 17th century, and with it began the hierarchization of the various aspects of the machinic. The constriction of the terminological landscape also ushered in the increasing marginalization and metaphorization of all other meanings by the technical connotation. In this era there was a proliferation of metaphors of man as machine, of the state as machine, of the world as machine: with the introduction of a universal metaphor for a utilitarian and functional order on both the micro and the macro level, the functional and organizational mode of human organs, communal living, even the entire cosmos were to be explained with the constricted technical concept of the machine.

Yet deep in the 19th century there was already an indication of the de-/re-coding of the machine concept that was then to be completely actualized in the

20th century. Beyond the poles of increasingly exact calculations for the economic functionalization of technical machines on the one hand and social-romantic Luddism on the other, at the same time that the Industrial Revolution finally spread all over Europe there was an unmistakable movement in the direction that would lead to generalized machine thinking in the second half of the 20th century: in the "Fragment on Machines," a section of *Grundrisse der Kritik der politischen Ökonomie*, drafted in 1857–58, Karl Marx developed his ideas on the transformation of the means of labor from a simple tool into a form corresponding to fixed capital, in other words into technical machines and "machinery."

In general, Marx sees the machine succinctly as a "means for producing surplus-value," in other words certainly not intended to reduce the labor effort of the workers, but rather to optimize their exploitation. Marx describes this function of "machinery" in Chapter 13 of *Das Kapital* with the three aspects of enhancing the human being utilizable as labor power (especially women's and child labor), prolonging the working day and intensifying labor. In the "Fragment on Machines" Marx focuses especially on the historical development that he (and others) described, at the end of which the machine, unlike the tool, is not at all to be understood as a means of labor for the individual worker: instead it encloses the knowledge and skill of workers and scholars as objectified knowledge and skill, opposing the workers scattered in its plane of immanence as a dominant and central power. From this perspective the modes of subjectivation and socialization are certainly not to be regarded as the outside of the machine (and thus to be constructed as machine metaphors), but rather as enclosed in the technical machinery.

Marx describes the relationship between humans and machines primarily as *social subjection*, as the intervention of the machine as an alien force in the living labor of the scattered workers, who—"subsumed under the overall process of the machinery itself"—function as parts of a mechanical system, as living accessories to this machinery, as means of its action. Here Marx seems to follow the pair of metaphors depicting the machine as a gigantic organism and the human beings as its dependent, appropriated components. Capital develops in this as power over living labor that has "subjected itself to the production process as a whole."

The automatic system of machinery that seems to be set in motion by a "moving force that moves itself," this automaton, however, is not imagined even by Marx in the Machine Fragment as a purely technical apparatus, as a purely anorganic, non-living composition, but rather as "consisting of numerous mechanical and intellectual organs." The workers operating the apparatuses are just as much a part of the machine as the intellectual, cognitive labor of those who have developed the machine and make up its social environment: economists, managers, and engineers. Marx thus formulates on the one hand the separation of the workers from their means of work, their determination through the machines, the domination of living labor by objectified labor, and introduces the figure of the inverse relationship of humans and machines: from the machine as a means for the human being to ease his or her working and living conditions to the human being as a means of the machine. From this perspective, human action on the machine, ultimately limited to preserving the machine from disruptions, is thoroughly subjected to the order of the machinery and not the other way around. Even the immaterial, intellectual, cognitive work that consisted in developing the machine, due to its enclosure in the technical apparatus, becomes an alien, extra-human power of the machine on the human components acting in the machine.

The reversal of the relationship of workers and means of labor in the direction of the domination of the machine over the human being is not only defined through the linear development from the tool to the composite technical apparatus and through the hierarchy in the labor process, but also as the inversion of power over knowledge. In the logic of social subjection, it seems that "all sciences are imprisoned in service to capital." Through the process of objectifying all forms of knowledge in the machine, the producers of this knowledge lose the undivided competency and the power over the labor process; living labor itself regards itself on the one hand as objectified, dead labor in the machine, on the other as scattered, divided among single living workers at many points in the machinery.

Yet even for Marx in the Machine Fragment, the enormous, self-active machine is more than a mechanism. The machine is not at all limited to its technical aspects, but is instead a mechanical-intellectual, even social assemblage: although technology and knowledge (as machine) have a one-sided impact on the workers, the machine is a concatenation not only of technology and knowledge, of the mechanical and the intellectual, but also and beyond this of social "organs," at least to the extent that it carries out the coordination of the scattered workers. What is evident in this, first of all, is an anticipation of the double relationship of *social subjection* and *machinic enslavement*: the machine not only forms its subjects, it structuralizes and striates not only the workers as an automaton, as an apparatus, as a structure, as a purely technical machine in the final stage of the development of the means of labor; it is also permeated by mechanical, intellectual and social "organs," which not only drive and operate it, but also successively develop, renew and even invent it.

The machine, however, also generates a flash of overcoming this double relationship of social subjection and machinic enslavement, hence the possible, if not the necessary collectivity of the human intellect. In a well-known passage of the Fragment, Marx opens up this potentiality with the concept of the *general intellect* which later became, especially for Italian Operaism and Postoperaism, the common point of reference for an emancipatory turn in machine theory: machines "are *organs of the human brain, created by the human hand;* the power of knowledge, objectified. The development of fixed capital indicates to what degree general social knowledge has become a *direct force of production*, and to what degree, hence, the conditions of the process of social life itself have come under the control of the general intellect and been transformed in accordance with it. To what degree the powers of social production have been produced, not only in the form of knowledge, but also as immediate organs of social practice, of the real life process."

The Fragment on Machines not only points to the fact that knowledge and skill are accumulated and absorbed in fixed capital as "general productive forces of the social brain" and that the process of turning production into knowledge is a tendency of capital, but also indicates the inversion of this tendency: the concatenation of knowledge and technology is not exhausted in fixed capital, but also refers beyond the technical machine and the knowledge objectified in it, to forms of social cooperation and communication, not only as machinic enslavement, but also as the capacity of immaterial labor—and this form of labor, as especially (post-) Operaist theory would later insist, can destroy the conditions under which accumulation develops. Marx at least writes in the Fragment on Machines that forces of production and social relations are the material conditions to blow the foundation of capital sky-high …

As early as the 19th century, a machinic thinking emerged which actualized the concatenation of technical apparatuses with social assemblages and with the intellect as a collective capacity, and recognizes revolutionary potentials in this. In multiple waves and in different fields and disciplines, now the process of narrowing and disambiguating the machine as a technical machine, which has predominated for over three hundred years, is turning around again. The long linear history of the expansion of the hand as a serving means of labor to the hand operating technical apparatuses (in which the hand itself becomes a prosthesis of the apparatus) to the complete autonomy of the machine and the subjection of the human being loses its significance. To the extent that it is not limited to the designation of technical apparatuses, the concept of the machine no longer refers only to a metaphor of the mechanic functioning of something other than technical machines. Although these kinds of ideas still remain dominant, they are being increasingly supplanted by a thinking that grasps the technical machine conversely as an indication of a more general notion of the machine behind it. From the excessive literary machine fantasies of Futurism, Constructivism and Surrealism through the cybernetics and socio-cybernetics of not only Norbert Wiener and the increasingly expanding research on the machine in the philosophy of science, for instance by Canguilhem and Simondon, there is an ongoing intensification of an extensive understanding of the machine reaching all the way to the cyborg theories of Donna Haraway and the Cyberfeminist International around the last turn of the century. However, this development is not to be regarded as a solely historical-linear one, from the pre-modern extension of the machine concept through modern demarcations to these boundaries finally becoming permeable (again and in a different way), but is instead also to be examined in the respective historical context of its movement.

In Félix Guattari's writings, especially what he wrote in the 1970s together with Gilles Deleuze, this movement is expanded and condensed: the technical machine is declared a subset of a more comprehensive machinic issue and terminology, which is opened up to the outside and to its machinic environment and maintains all kinds of relationships to social components and subjectivities.[1] It thus thwarts, first of all, the opposition of man and machine, of organism and mechanism developed over the course of centuries, on the basis of which one is explained by the other, the human from the machine or the machine from the human, in both anthropocentric and mechanistic world views. Both, although they seem to be in extreme opposition, see themselves in the conventional linear paradigms, even in the thwarting of their dichotomy as unbroken, without resistance, instrumental: mechanism and organism share the ideal notion of an endless, empty repetition without difference, of an overall functionality and of a rigorous subjection of the parts.

----

1. At this point it should be noted that the way Guattari and Deleuze use the concept of the machine is thoroughly ambivalent. The shadow sides of machinization regularly appear, such as in the reflections on fascist and post-fascist forms of the war machine in *A Thousand Plateaus*, or in Guattari's 1980s concept of "machinic enslavement" in "worldwide integrated capitalism," as he called the phenomenon framed today as globalization. "Machinic enslavement" does not mean here simply the subordinated relationship of the human being to the social knowledge of objectifying technical machines, but rather a more general form of the collective administration of knowledge and the necessity of permanent, even if seemingly self-determined, participation. The machinic quality of postfordist capitalism appends to the traditional systems of direct oppression—and here Guattari is very close to the theories of neoliberal governmentality developed by Foucault—a range of control mechanisms requiring the complicity of individuals.

In contrast, for Deleuze and Guattari the (desiring) machine is only to be found in the simultaneity of flow and rupture. Human bodies collapse, technical apparatuses become dysfunctional or are brought to a halt with the wooden shoe of sabotage, states crumble in civil war or are evacuated in exodus. Yet the orgiastic paradigm of *Anti-Oedipus* does not foreground the human being, the technical apparatus, the state, but rather the relationship between the streams and ruptures of assemblages, in which organic, technical and social machines are concatenated.

In the "Appendix" to *Anti-Oedipus* Gilles Deleuze and Félix Guattari not only develop a "Balance Sheet Program for Desiring Machines," but also write their own machine concept, in undisguised, yet initially not explicit contrast to Marx's ideas on machinery. This involves an expansion or renewal of the concept, first of all against metaphorizing the machine. Deleuze and Guattari do not want to establish another "figurative sense" of the machine, but instead attempt to newly invent the term at a critical distance from both the everyday sense and Marxist scholars. Marx's machine theory (although not the machine theory from *Grundrisse* discussed above, but rather the less fragmentary, but theoretically smoother one from *Das Kapital*) is introduced here with the cipher "that classical scheme," but explicitly named only in the third and final part of the appendix. In the thirteenth chapter of *Das Kapital*, Marx addressed at some length the distinction between tool and machine, specifically under the aspect of how a means of labor is transformed from a tool (which Guattari calls a proto-machine) into a machine. With this he repeated the straight line from tools of the human organism to tools of a technical apparatus that he had already outlined in *The Misery of Philosophy*. This linear conception is criticized by Deleuze/Guattari as insufficient in many respects. They question less the immanent logic of the transformation of machines as described by Marx, but rather the framework that Marx presupposes as the basis of this logic: a dimension of man and nature common to all social forms. The linear development from tool (as an extension of the human being to relieve strain) toward an upheaval, in the course of which the machine ultimately becomes independent of the human being, so to speak, simultaneously determines the machine as one aspect in a mechanical series. This kind of schema, "stemming from the humanist spirit and abstract," especially isolates the productive forces from the social conditions of their application. Deleuze and Guattari hence shift the perspective from the question of the form in which the machine follows simpler tools, how humans and tools become machinized, to the question of which social machines make the occurrence of specific technical, affective, cognitive, semiotic machines and their concatenations possible and necessary.

Beyond evolutive schemes, the machine is no longer only a function in a series imagined as starting from the tool, which occurs at a certain point. Similar to the way the *techne* and *mechané* concepts of antiquity already meant both material object and practice, the machine is also not solely an instrument of work, in which social knowledge is absorbed and enclosed. Instead it opens up in respectively different social contexts to different concatenations, connections and couplings.

Instead of placing tool and machine in a series, Deleuze and Guattari seek a more fundamental differentiation of the two concepts. As in the following section of this text, this distinction can be described in the form of a different genealogy than the sequence from tool to machine, namely one that takes recourse to the pre-modern understanding of the *machina*. In *Anti-Oedipus*, however, this difference is treated conceptually/theoretically: the machine is a communication factor, the tool—at least in its non-machinic form—is, on the other hand, a communicationless extension or prosthesis. Conversely, the concrete tool in its use for exchange/connection with the human being is always more machine than the technical machine imagined in isolation. For Deleuze and Guattari, becoming a piece with something else means something fundamentally different from extending oneself, projecting oneself or being replaced by a technical apparatus.

By distinguishing the machine from something that simply extends or replaces the human being,

Deleuze and Guattari not only refuse to affirm the simple cultural-pessimism figure of the machine's domination over the human being. They also posit a difference from an all too simplistic and optimistic celebration of a certain form of machine, which from Futurism to cyber-fans is in danger of overlooking the social aspect in ever new combinations of "man-machine." Technical prostheses as a sheer endless extension of the inadequate human being, fictions of artificial humans following Mary Shelley's Frankenstein, stories of machines increasingly penetrating into the human being usually prove to be reductionist complements to the paradigm of alienation. The narrative of man's becoming-machine as a purely technical alteration misses the machinic, both in its civilization-critical development and in its euphoric tendency. It is no longer a matter of confronting man and machine to estimate possible or impossible correspondences, extensions and substitutions of the one or the other, of ever new relationships of similarity and metaphorical relations between humans and machines, but rather of concatenations, of how man becomes a piece with the machine or with other things in order to constitute a machine. The "other things" may be animals, tools, other people, statements, signs or desires, but they only become machine in a process of exchange, not in the paradigm of substitution.

According to Guattari, the primary characteristic of the machine is the flowing of its components: every extension or substitution would be communication-lessness, and the quality of the machine is exactly the opposite, namely that of communication, of exchange. Contrary to the structure (and to the later conceptualized double of the structure, the state apparatus), which tends toward closure, the machinic corresponds to a tendentially permanent praxis of connection. From the text "Machine and Structure," written in 1969, to "Machinic heterogenesis," published in 1991, a year before his death, Guattari repeatedly pointed out the different quality of machine and structure, machine and state apparatus. The machine is not limited to managing and striating entities closed off to one another, but opens up to other machines and, together with them, moves machinic assemblages. It consists of machines and penetrates several structures simultaneously. It depends on external elements in order to be able to exist at all. It implies a complementarity not only with the human being that fabricates it, allows it to function or destroys it, but also exists in itself in a relationship of difference and exchange with other virtual or actual machines.

If we want to continue to approach a machine concept that is as extensive as it is ambivalent, then the historical context of Guattari's writings should also be included in our considerations. Which question does the concept of the machine answer here, which problem does it actualize? What is the reason for the intricate endeavor to tear the everyday machine concept from its commonplace connotation? Guattari had already started to develop his machine concept in the late 1960s, specifically against the background of micropolitical experiences and leftist experiments in organizing. These endeavors were initially directed against the hard segmentarity of Real-Socialist and Euro-Communist state left-wings, against the process of the structuralization of revolutionary movements also and particularly among the left; they were then further explored on the basis of the experiences of diverse subcultural and micropolitical practices, in Guattari's case especially on the basis of the anti-psychiatric practice of institutional analysis in the La Borde clinic. They ultimately flowed, even after 1968, into efforts to resist and reflect on the structuralization and closure of the 1968 generation in cadres, factions and circles.

The problem that Guattari deals with in his first machine text, written briefly after the experience of 1968, is the problem of a lasting revolutionary organization, an instituent machine that should guarantee that it does not close itself off in the various social structures, especially not in the state structure. From this perspective, Guattari's extensive machine concept is a strategy for opposing the machine to the danger of structuralization and state-apparatization, as well as against the identitary closing effects of concepts of community: the machine as a non-identitary concept for fleeing stratification and identification, for inventing new forms of the concatenation of singularities.

3

THEATER MACHINES

The body is a machine, the worker a machinist.
— V.E. Meyerhold

The machinist is part of the machine, not only in his activity as machinist, but also afterwards.
— Gilles Deleuze/Félix Guattari, *Kafka. Towards a Minor Literature*

The work on scenic material, the transformation of the stage into a machine, which helps to develop the work of the actor as broadly and manifoldly as possible, is then socially justified when this machine not only moves its pistons and holds up under a certain work load, but also begins to carry out a certain useful labour.
— Sergei Tretyakov, *The Theater of Attractions*

The primary material of the theater will turn out to be the viewer … Tool for working on all the components of the theater apparatus…, which in all their differentness can be returned to a unit that legitimizes their existence, which is their character of attraction… I define an attraction in the formal sense as a self-reliant and primary construction element of a performance—as the molecular (i.e. constitutive) element of the effectiveness of theater and of theater itself.
— Sergei Eisenstein, *Montage of Attractions*

The term *machina* has appeared in Latin since Plautus and Ennius in the early second century B.C. and increasingly during the imperial era and late antiquity, initially as a loan word from the Doric vocabulary of the colonists of lower Italy. The Latin *machina* thus assumes all the meanings of the Greek *mechané* (the Doric word, already relatively close to the Latin, was *machaná*). Its more general meaning as "means, contrivance, device" does not further distinguish between material and immaterial means, but instead allows them to overlap and merge. This basic extension of the term between a material device and a contriving approach, and especially the many overlaps of both aspects remain its characteristic in most languages in which it has developed over the course of modernity. In ancient Greek and Latin the term spread primarily into two fields of application—the significance of this for Guattari's and Deleuze's machine concept is not to be underestimated. On the one hand there was the military use as an apparatus for besieging, conquering or defending cities, in other words as a war machine, while on the other hand it was also used as a comprehensive term for the machinery of the theater.

This bifurcation into the fields of war and theater, however, does not imply a separation into the material and the immaterial meaning along the boundaries of these two fields. In both cases of application the term both holds the technical meaning of apparatuses, frames, devices as well as the psychosocial meaning of trick, artifice, deception. This ambiguity is most adequately transported in English by the word "invention" (from Latin *invenio* meaning "to find, to come upon"): the machine is an invention, an invented device, and it is an "invention" as an invented story, as a deception, as a machination. Technical innovation and inventiveness blur together here along the two mutually merging lines of the meaning of machine.

This kind of neighboring zone between the double artifice of technical art and artistic creation developed for the first time in the period of the zenith of Greek drama in the fifth century B.C. In the theater of antiquity, machine meant primarily the deity machine, the *theòs epì mechanés*, the *deus ex machina*. The *mechané*, or later in Roman theater the *machina*, was the general term for all stage machines, such as thunder and lightning machines or devices for making the dead vanish into the underworld. However, *the* machine of the Attic theater was a specific device placed above the left stage door. All the gods and heroes of the air appeared on this left side, so they had to be lowered to the stage from above. The actors playing deities probably hung from a hook fastened to the belt, which was in turn attached with a rope to a system of rolls or pulleys. With the help of this machine a god or goddess thus appeared from above, assuming a special function within the plot of the play: he or she was to resolve all the aporia that had emerged in the course of the play. Euripides especially used this technique in a double sense (as narrative technique and as apparatus technique): a sudden resolution of all the complications that had arisen in the course of the plot that seemed hopeless and immanently irresolvable, with the help of a crane-like machine that allowed gods, goddesses and other figures to fly onto the stage or even the proscenium or the roof of the stage.

Deus ex machina meant the development of theater technique as a machination and machinery, yet at the same time it was also an artistic effect, a trick, a break, a sudden twist capable of resolving complex entanglements in the plot all at once. Its function was to resolve the most abstruse confusions, which developed in the dramatic subject matter of the late fifth century. The very cunning invention of complications that could not easily be disentangled and their artificial resolution through the *deus ex machina* were presumably connected with the political disturbances and impositions of the Peloponnesian War, and the fairy-tale-like happy end through the *deus ex machina* in Euripides' later tragedies was understood as a comforting, yet clearly artificial suspension of difficult circumstances. At the end of a plot, in which, unlike in the tragedies of his predecessors Aeschylus and Sophocles, the gods no longer determine the scene from the beginning to the end, in other words a plot that moves almost solely in the human sphere, a god does still appear in Euripides' plays. In *Iphigenia in Tauris*, the flight of Iphigenia and Orestes at first succeeds through human insight and cunning, then finally—following a sudden surge of the sea—through an intervention from the goddess Athena. In *Ion*, following a long period of uncertainty about his origin and the interplay of attraction and intrigues between Ion and his mother Creusa, it is due less to the interventions of his father Apollo than to an epiphany of Athena that Ion is introduced into the Athenian royal family. In *Helen*, Menelaus and Helen are rescued from Egypt through their own cunning, but mostly through the help of Castor and Pollux; in *Orestes*, it is due to the ingenuity of Orestes and Electra and to the *deus ex machina* Apollo that the pair reach a happy end. In each case there is the same pattern of the sympathetic description of the protagonists' misfortunes in the opening scenes, the development of complex intrigues, of *mechánema*, the main figures themselves employing ideas for escape and cunning inventions, and finally a surprising climax of the saving intervention by the *deus ex machina*. Instead of the turbulent conflicts of various gods in a heterogeneous landscape of deities (whether hierarchically ruled by the father-god Zeus or a quasi anarchic setting of manifold deities), the *deus ex machina* embodies singular and sovereign protection by a single autonomous deity.

It was Aristotle who first criticized this use of gods on suspension and flying machines in his *Poetics*, affirming that the resolution of the story should result from the story itself and not through a *deus ex machina*. Instead, divine interventions should only be represented in the meta-situations that lie outside the stage plot, which have occurred before or after it, in other words in prologues and epilogues. This general rule in Aristotle's *Poetics* makes the *deus ex machina* of Euripides's tragedies look like an expedient device for a mediocre playwright, necessary for disentangling the dramatic knots he has created, but which virtually take on a life of their own. What is overlooked in an interpretation like this, however, is the skillfulness with which these knots are often constructed, so that in the end only a goddess can untie them. At least in the case of Euripides' late tragedies, the epiphany of the *deus ex machina* is not so much a makeshift solution, as it is a purposely and carefully constructed crosspoint and climax of technical spectacle and the invention of intrigues.

It was possibly Aristotle's criticism in antiquity that forestalled an unbroken theater genealogy of the machine-god over the centuries, and which still echoes in Nietzsche's assessment of the *deus ex machina* as a sign of the downfall of tragedy. In this long modern development of the theater, the double function of the *deus ex machina* as interrupting apparatus and break of the narrative is increasingly displaced.

The rupture, the break, the obvious artificiality of the machine is interpreted as an unartistic act of force and therefore has to be covered up more and more. To an ever greater degree machines serve a rapid change of scenery and the perfect illusion, the smoothing of breaks. The cloud machines of the Italian baroque theater, for instance, had not only the function of transporting and illuminating deities, but also and especially of masking the technical apparatuses.

In the interests of the bourgeois theater of illusion, technical devices and narrative machinations equally serve to covertly suspend the different in identity, when the specificity of the sudden break, of surprise and confusion gives way to the harmonious resolution at the conclusion of the play. Whereas with Euripides the artificiality, the intended inconsistency, the unreality of the happy end was evident, the organic suspensions of modern theater tend to lead to a distanceless empathy. This theater, as it says in *Anti-Oedipus*, "forces the play and the working of machines into the wings, behind a limit that has become impassible." When Brecht in 1928 explicitly designated the final scene of the *Three-Penny Opera* with the title *deus ex machina*, it was only to call attention again to this problem of the bourgeois theater: undisturbed enjoyment of untenable situations that can only in theater be resolved by a riding messenger. With the naming of the *deus ex machina*, Brecht emphasized the artificiality of suspending the conflicts and differences (that were not to be tamed immanently) into transcendentality: "The riding messengers of the king rarely come when those kicked have kicked back."

Post-revolutionary theater in the Soviet Union of the early 1920s substantially influenced (not only) Brecht as the climax of the flight from hiding the machines and machinations to inventing new interrupting apparatuses and narrative breaks, which went far beyond the singular appearance of the *deus ex machina*. The October Revolution was accompanied by the vehement question of revolutionizing art, including the bourgeois theater. Should the theater of the scientific age emerge from a transformation of the bourgeois theater, or as a radical new beginning, or did the only solution consist in completely rejecting theater as a bourgeois practice? Those who decided, under the name "Theater October," in favor of solutions in between transformation and new beginning, increasingly dispensed with illusionist plots and the psychology of the figures, did away with the peep show stage, the curtain, the backdrops, built new theaters, left the theater. Instead of using the *machina* as a divine suspension of difference, the radical theater-makers associated with Meyerhold and the First Moscow Workers Theater were more interested in multiplying differences, making them dance with the help of a multiple machinization of concepts and practices. Here the machine was given its threefold composition as the biomechanics of the actors, as the constructivism of the technical apparatuses and things, and as the social machine of the Theater of Attractions. The machine material of the post-revolutionary Soviet theater encompassed the bodies of the actors, the construction, the audience: it anticipated the concatenation of human organs, technical apparatuses and social machines that constitute the machine for Deleuze and Guattari.

Following far-ranging experiments on *Commedia dell'arte* and on the traditional Russian circus genre of the Balagan in the 1910s in his Petersburg studio, which was simultaneously an acting school and a laboratory, in Moscow in the early 1920s, V.E. Meyerhold developed more than a new acting method; his method of biomechanics was a new, generalized theater pedagogy. "The body is a machine, the worker the machinist," according to Meyerhold, and this especially implied experimenting with all flows of movement. Against the background of an idiosyncratic appropriation of Taylorism, Meyerhold primarily began to rationalize the apparatus of movement: the body of the actors as model for a generalized optimization of movements, the biomechanical experiment as a model for the potential utilization in labor processes outside the realm of the theater. Yet under the mantle of the Taylorist vocabulary and a seemingly overzealous utilitarianism, Meyerhold and his colleagues carried out experiments little touched by the problems of the scientific organization of labor and the creation of a New (Soviet) Man: They aimed at denaturalizing the theater.

Contrary to the psychology of the plot and to an empathetic audience, the core components of biomechanics were the rhythm of language and the rhythm of physical movement, postures and gestures arising from these rhythms, coordinating the movement of the body and bodies with one another. The development of the plot was not to come from "within," from the psyche or mind, but rather "from outside," through the movement of the body in space. These components were created through an economy of means of expression, control of bodies and gestures, precision and tempo of movement, speed of reaction and improvisation. Meyerhold's acting school was not merely a school for gymnastics and acrobatics, but rather attempted to bring the actors to calculate and coordinate their movements before that and beyond it, to organize their material, to organize the body.

As a first larger presentation of biomechanics, *The Magnanimous Cuckold*, a contemporary play by the Belgian author Fernand Crommelynck, premiered in April 1922. Sculptural images of bodies and movements, athletics and rhythm permeated the scenes. The stage was open far to the back, all the way to the brick wall, all the stage machinery was transparent. The performance thus became the first concatenation of biomechanics and constructivism:

as much as Meyerhold separated the bodies of his actors in training and treated them individually as material, just as little did he forget the machinic environment of these bodies, the things, the objects, the materials and constructions on the stage. In a rapid succession of treatments and new plays, in collaboration with constructivist artists he also created a theater of things that no longer sought pure representations and images, but instead to present the things themselves. Instead of an illusionist stage set, instead of props and stage decorations, artists like Liubov Popova and Varvara Stepanova invented and designed constructions, prototypes, handled objects, which were placed for use on an otherwise empty stage. In this movement of inventing, (re-) arranging and reappropriating things, technical apparatuses, and stage construction, the theater machinery also moved from the practice of being most skillfully hidden back into the light of perception.

The scenery for *The Magnanimous Cuckold*, constructed by Liubov Popova, was no longer actually scenery, but was instead a single machine made of planks, ramps, ladders and scaffolds. In analogy to this, there were no costumes either, but rather uniform blue suits also designed by Popova. The actors moved around the stage not only horizontally, but also vertically, climbing, exercising, sliding, using Popova's machine as the frame for their movements.

In the next biomechanical-constructivist piece by the Meyerhold Theater, *Tarelkin's Death*, Varvara Stepanova chopped up the machine into many objects, which she called "apparatuses," small and large, mobile furniture mock-ups. The actors were able to apply and expand their biomechanical skills in handling these apparatuses and constructivist devices.

The transformation of the stage into a machine, the work on scenic material was—as Sergei Tretyakov explained in his fundamental essay on the "Theater of Attractions"—only "then socially justified when this machine not only moves its pistons and holds up under a certain work load, but also begins to carry out a certain useful labor and meets the ongoing daily tasks of the Revolution." In Tretyakov's radical treatment of Marcel Martinet's *La Nuit*, which premiered February 1923 on the fifth anniversary of the founding of the Red Army under the title *Earth Rampant* in the Meyerhold Theater, Liubov Popova placed real machines on the stage instead of constructions. Along with photos and posters, her combination of collage and construction also included rifles, machine guns, cannons, motorcycles and even a military truck. The *polit-revue* about World War I and the beginning of the Russian Revolution was extremely successful and was performed over a hundred times just in 1923. To a certain extent, *Earth Rampant* still belonged to the tradition of the mass plays of war communism, the re-stagings of the October Revolution and Mayakovsky's

Mysterium buffo, but at the same time it also created a transition to the Theater of Attractions, which emerged in Tretyakov's collaboration with the young Sergei Eisenstein and marked the climax of machinic theater production of the 1920s.

Before the period of major film productions, it was left up to this young Eisenstein, who had still worked as assistant director on *Tarelskin's Death*, to realize Meyerhold's plans as the exodus of the theater into the factory, as the concatenation of constructivist stage sets with technical machines. In 1924, in the third and final theater cooperation of Eisenstein and Tretyakov, *Gas Masks*, the everyday life of the factory was at the center not only of the plot: the first performances were organized in gas works at the Minsk train station and performed before an exclusive audience of workers. Wooden scaffolds were built for the actors in between the monumental superstructures of the factory, in the midst of which they acted. Tretyakov had taken the subject matter of *Gas Masks* from a news article in *Pravda*. According to this article, after an accident seventy workers from a gas work in the Ural region had taken action themselves, collectively and at the risk of their lives, to repair a leak in the main gas pipe, each working for three minutes on the main pipe without a gas mask and thereby enduring poisoning. The theatrical treatment of the self-organized and collective action was intended to examine what the future of labor could look like, based on an emergency, an event, an impending disaster in the midst of the difficult political transition phase following the Revolution. At the same time, this model was no longer anchored in the glorious periods of the battles on the barricades, the Revolution, but rather in the everyday life of the factory and the difficulties of production. The immanent criticism of the sloppy NEP director of the gas works in the play, who had repeatedly postponed obtaining gas masks, corresponds to Eisenstein and Tretyakov's actual flight from the theater. The reason for their exodus from the theater was not only the glorious Proletkult idea of "culture for all," but also the simple and sober insight that its audience was increasingly interspersed with the Nouveau Riche of the NEP. In the factory as well, however, the theater activists soon realized that they were no more than tolerated, and they left again after four performances. For Eisenstein, this movement of flight from the theater consequentially ended not in the factory, but instead led him on to film.

It had already become clearly evident a year earlier that biomechanics and constructivism had not yet gone far enough in precisely investigating the material of the machine. They had to expand the machine concept from the body-machines of the actors and the machine constructions on the stage to the *social machine*, which stretched beyond the protagonists on the stage to a diffuse and illimitable assemblage: it was the viewers that should finally be inflamed by the trained elastic actor-machine and the constructivist apparatuses. The experiments of the radical leftist artists in the brief golden age of the Theater of Attractions in 1923/24 did not take the direction of the dissolution of art and life, as in the large-scale mass spectacles of the post-revolutionary period, but rather the direction of developing specific competences of the actors as well as a specific audience. This was accompanied by a precise assessment of the relationship between stage and audience space, actors and audience.

In the course of Meyerhold's experiments in Petersburg and Moscow, a special form of segmenting the scenic action into small units, acrobatic "numbers," and rapid slapstick sequences had been developed. In addition to Meyerhold's experiments in the 1910s, the early futurist theater experiments by Vladimir Mayakovsky, Velimir Chlebnikov and Alexei Kruchenykh, but also the Dadaist excesses in Western Europe were crucial for the Theater of Attractions. However, whereas the Dadaist farces took place in the marginal setting of places like the Cabaret Voltaire, the theater of the leftist Proletkult brought the circus, the fair acrobatics, and the attraction into the official theater of the young state of the Soviet Union. Tretyakov and Eisenstein called their Soviet variation the "Theater of Attractions," thus inventing a molecular concatenation of single, independent attractions with their aggressive moments and risky action processes. In analogy to the fragmentary compositions of Heartfield, Grosz and Rodchenko, they transformed the static theater of depiction and of milieu description into a dynamic and eccentric theater, deconstructed the molar-organic linearity of the theater plot and mounted the attractions into an orgiastic molecularity. The fragmentation of the plot, its segmentation into attractions, raised the question of a new form of the concatenation of attractions, of a montage that should treat the social machine in their sense. Eisenstein stressed that the attraction was intended to be the opposite of the absolute and the complete, especially because it was based exclusively on something relative, on the reaction of the audience.

Whereas Meyerhold still regarded the body of the actor as material and as machine, Eisenstein's material/machine was the audience. Sergei Eisenstein started his position as artistic director at the First Workers' Theater Moscow with the theoretical essay "Montage of Attractions" and a piece designated as such. As with Meyerhold's adaptation of *La Nuit*, Eisenstein commissioned Tretyakov with a radical treatment. In the infight with the right-wing currents of the Proletkult, it was particularly provocative to take up a popular comedy of intrigues by the classically naturalist dramatist Ostrovsky, *Enough Stupidity in Every Wise Man*—and to distort it until it became completely unrecognizable. The program booklet accordingly stated: "Free text composition: S.M. Tretyakov, Scenario S.M. Eisenstein." *The Wise Man* premiered in May 1923. The audience sat in a semicircle in two amphitheaters divided by a narrow passage. Instead of a stage, the floor in front of the amphitheaters formed a circus ring with various devices, scaffolds and ropes. The attractions were strung together as breathtaking acrobatic feats and tricks, which required the actors' entire biomechanical skills, yet at the same time parodied the canonized performance practices in the theater and in the circus. In addition to acrobatics in the air and on the ground, clowns, rope dancing and eccentric musical numbers, Eisenstein's first short film was also shown.

As in Meyerhold's pseudo-Taylorist procedures, in the Theater of Attractions tension and audience attacks were also coupled with a gesture of the precise scientific investigation of the audience. Not only discussions after the performances were to be part of a meticulous procedure for calculating the effects and the attitude of the audience, but also participating observation, questionnaires and an exact documentation of expressions from the audience during the performances. What started in 1922 as a planned fragmentation of bourgeois theater, however, had developed by 1925 into an increasingly grotesque discussion in art studies circles: in Meyerhold's theater the audience was more and more compulsively observed and degraded to a research object. In a harshly utilitarian and behavioristic perspective, the plays were fragmented into small units of time and the audience reactions were charted according to twenty standard reactions. From silence all the way to throwing things onto the stage, those responsible registered everything down to the smallest detail. This method of real-time evaluation was intended to supply insights for new productions, but it led instead to more of a state apparatization of the theater. Through the notation not only of audience reactions, but also of all aspects of production (from the actors and stage personnel to the bookkeeping), it was possible to immediately find fault with mistakes and omissions. The fetish of "scientific calculation" developed into a comprehensive control system. Internal rationality, joining the parts into the whole, panoptic survey: all the components of the ideal of the purely technical machine formed the ideal state apparatus.

In some of Eisenstein and Tretyakov's texts, it also appears at first as though the linear progression from the political goal of the theater to societal effect dominates to such an extent that one could speak here of an overcoding of the machines by the state apparatus, perhaps even of a glimpse of the Stalinist politics of a totalitarian "purge." This diction, however, is mainly determined by the contemporary jargon in the years following the Revolution and later by the incipient censorship of theater operations and the cultural political discourse following the introduction of the NEP. This was additionally disambiguated and closed in the one-sided historicization by later art and theater studies (both in the Soviet Union and in the "West"), which excluded phenomena deviating from the doctrine of Social Realism from their narratives. In comparison, in Eisenstein and Tretyakov's plays a parody can be recognized of the simple, linear notions of agitation, which are based on the pseudo-sociological screening of class composition and sought to optimize its effects without deviations. Eisenstein and Tretyakov did not construct the audience as an object, but instead specifically attempted to provide an impulse for trying out new modes of subjectivation. When they spoke of the audience as "material," this was in analogy to Meyerhold's relationship to the biomechanical body, and the point was the experimental build-up of tension, the organization of the social arrangement into self-organization. The montage of attractions conjoined singularities as human, technical and social bodies in an unexpected way, thwarting the horizons of expectations and ultimately supplied material for eruption and tumult.

Half a year after the *Wise Man*, Tretyakov and Eisenstein brought a politicized version of their Montage of Attractions into the Proletkult Theater. On the sixth anniversary of the Revolution, on 7

November 1923, Tretyakov's play *Can You Hear, Moscow?!* opened. Subtitled as "Agit-Guignol," it was intended to link agitation with the device of horror (following the practice of the Paris theater *Grand Guignol*). As a logical development of politicization from the formal experiment with "abstract" attractions in the *Wise Man* to political agitation, it was animated by a concrete agitational mission: Tretyakov had written the play as a propaganda play and action to mobilize volunteers from Moscow for the anticipated revolution in Germany—which failed from the start due to the historical developments. The plot: a provincial governor with the significant name Graf Stahl (Count Steel) wants to stage a patriotic fair as a counter-staging to expected proletarian demonstrations on the anniversary of the October Revolution. He plans to present a historical play and the festivities are to culminate in the unveiling of a statue of an 'Iron Count,' mythical ancestor of Graf Stahl. However, stage workers and actors change the play. Following increasingly clear allusions to phenomena of exploitation, a gigantic portrait of Lenin is unveiled, which incites the armed revolt. Heroic exploited people, martyrs and revolutionaries on one side, caricatured exploiters and their ideologues, provocateurs and conformist social democrats on the other. The climax of the play (not only the play in the play) celebrates the upheaval that leads out of the theater into life. At the end of the plot a protagonist agitates the Moscow audience with the words: "Can you hear, Moscow?!" And according to the script, the audience is to respond unanimously: "Yes, I hear!" What actually happened, was obviously something different. The tumultuous excess on the stage so inflamed especially the youthful audience and the extras that the actors playing the bourgeois were attacked even during the play; following the conclusion of *Can You Hear, Moscow?!*, the emotionalized audience purportedly poured into the streets in tumultuous scenes, singing and "wildly flailing against the shop windows."

For Tretyakov and Eisenstein, the evaluation of these real effects of their performance on the anniversary of the October Revolution turned out to be quite ambivalent and self-critical. Yet nevertheless, it represented a predictable consequence of the experiments of machinic theater in the early 1920s: it was the program of the Theater of Attractions to develop a form that turns emotions into extreme tension, in order to ultimately achieve a "release of the audience's emotions" (Tretyakov) through the montage of these attractions. Whereas the machinery and machination of the early *deus ex machina* turned the action of the theater play from the organic into the orgiastic, the threefold concatenation of the post-revolutionary machines was to intervene in the world, creating worlds instead of a representation of the world. The montage of physical movements in biomechanics, the montage of things and technical apparatuses in the constructivist stage settings, the montage of the audience as a social machine in the productivist Theater of Attractions sought not only a composition of organic, technical and social machines, but also the becoming-orgiastic of the organs, the flows of the technical constructions, the insurrection of the social machine.

4

WAR MACHINES

The war machine is that nomad invention that in fact has war not as its primary object but as its second-order, supplementary or synthetic objective, in the sense that it is determined in such a way as to destroy the State-form and city-form with which it collides.
— Gilles Deleuze/Félix Guattari, *A Thousand Plateaus*

The object of the war machine, as Deleuze and Guattari never tire of explaining in their "Treatise on Nomadology" in *A Thousand Plateaus*, is not simply war, but "the drawing of a creative line of flight, the composition of a smooth space and of the movement of people in that space." The weapons of this machine are nomadic lines of flight and invention. The combination of flight and invention, of the desertion from the state apparatus and the movement of instituting, the invention of an *instituent flight* is the specific quality of the war machine, in Deleuze's favorite formulation: "Fleeing, yes, but while fleeing looking for a weapon." The martial dimension of the war machine consists in the power of invention, in the capacity for change, in the creation of other worlds. It is only the appropriation by a state apparatus that can transform the war machine into a military apparatus, a war.

Some time ago I called the theater machine of the PublixTheatreCaravan a war machine, following from discourses in the genealogy of Walter Benjamin's essay on "The Critique of Violence" seeking to problematize the dichotomy of violence and non-violence. Referring to the Caravan not only as a theater machine, but also as a war machine was intended to actualize the overlapping of nomadism and the war machine developed by Deleuze and Guattari in the description of a micro-political, artistic-activist practice. To maintain that the Caravan—as I wrote at the time—operates on a line of flight, offensively as a war machine, does not at all mean attributing a special form of violence to it. On the contrary, the war machine points beyond the discourse of violence and terror, it is the machine that seeks to escape the violence of the state apparatus, the order of representation. Conversely, the state apparatus attempts to force the non-representable under the power of representation, for instance by making a Black Block out of the Caravan. I wrote that after the No-Border-Tour in the summer of 2001, which led from Vienna to the WEF summit in Salzburg and a border camp in Lendava to the G8 summit in Genoa, ending there with the arrest of most of the Caravan activists by the Italian police.

Several years later, in fall 2005, before a provincial court in the Upper Austrian town of Lambach, the striation and retreat of the war machine was repeated, but this time without the international flair of anti-G8 protests. The Caravan activists were charged with unauthorized assumption of authority and deception, because of an unannounced action in a school in Lambach (invisible agit-theater on the theme of bio-metrics) during the *Festival of the Regions* 2003, the theme of which was "The Art of Enmity." In this town-court farce, there was no trace left of attacks, offensives, of "searching for a weapon in fleeing," and I had to politely testify, limited to the role of an "art expert," that the action was a matter of art, that this form of art is established and recognized and that the artists certainly meant no harm to the children. As the Caravan activist Gini Müller once formulated in reference to the arrest of the PublixTheatreCaravan and the trials after Genoa: "The question of whether the line of flight is transversal or terrorist was to be judged by the molar tribunal."[1]

---

1. Gini Müller, "Transversal or Terror?," http://eipcp.net/transversal/0902/mueller/en. My essay was published as "A War-Machine against the Empire. On the precarious nomadism of the PublixTheatre-Caravan," http://eipcp.net/transversal/0902/raunig/en. On the history of the PublixTheatreCaravan (including Genoa and Strasbourg), cf. Gerald Raunig, *Art and Revolution*, Los Angeles: Semiotext(e), 2007, on the Lambach "biometrics trial," cf. http://lambach.volxtheater.at/.

The arrest and conviction of the Caravan thus reveals a different relationship between war machine and state apparatus than the one familiar from *A Thousand Plateaus*: in the "Treatise on Nomadology" Deleuze and Guattari describe how the state apparatus takes over the war machine, subordinates it to its own objectives and makes war its immediate purpose. In the appropriation of the war machine by the state apparatus, flight and invention ultimately do become war, the war machine becomes a (quasi) military apparatus. Perhaps the development of the phenomenon of the Black Block from Seattle 1999 to Rostock 2007 could be interpreted as this kind of process of appropriation. The development, in which the first mentions of the "black block" in the early 1980s started from the mediatization and criminalization of the autonomous activists in Germany, in which the images generated in the process were only secondarily—sometimes ironically, sometimes with deadly seriousness—taken over and affirmed by various fractions of the left, seems to have repeated itself in the last ten years with greater intensity: over the course of a brief decade, the construction of a block, which was initially mainly a media construction, both dichotomously and symmetrically opposed to the block of the Robocops increasingly lead to an actualization of this image and to the transformation of sections of the no-global war machine into a "war." State apparatuses (here, mainstream media and politics) generate "war" in the sense of a coerced integration of the war machine into a dually gridded order, in which the war machine itself (or its machist components) ultimately become a (quasi) military apparatus, a state apparatus.

The conceptual opposition (war) machine—the state apparatus must nevertheless be understood as a relationship of exchange, as an infinite multitude of possibilities of struggle, of mutual overlapping that develops various layers of coding and overcoding with their respective effects. In the extreme case of *Themroc*, for instance, two policemen as figures of the state apparatus are simply eaten in a process of anthropophagy. Yet even cannibalism is not to be understood as pure negation, but rather as a special relationship of the war machine Themroc to the ultimately ingested policemen. Themroc's gentle wildness and his comrades spreading out do not correspond to a mob that hurls itself at the state apparatus as a dense mass, as an agitated crowd (*Hetzmasse*, to use Elias Canetti's terminology), but rather as a formless, non-conforming assemblage, unreal and yet turning in a very corporeal way to the bodies of the others. Yet this assemblage is not unlike the diffuse one of the bicycle thieves, in which the Roman policemen seem to be incorporated in a completely different way. And even the eternity machine of *The Third Policeman* appropriates both his colleagues, who scurry around in the immeasurable space of the underground machine and operate it without a deeper understanding. The anarchical quality of the war machine, as is evident here again, seems to be equally on the side of resistance and of power, supporting capital as well as the flight from capitalism; it can be overcoded in a fascistoid way, but it can also generate emancipatory or even revolutionary flows. It is only the analysis of the specific relationship of war machines and state apparatuses that sheds light on the actualization of these ambivalences and the status of the respective appropriation.

The collision of the micropolitical praxis of the PublixTheatreCaravan with the state apparatus in Genoa and in Lambach is a different case. Here it is not a matter of appropriation, of machinic enslavement, of coding and overcoding, but rather an attempted annulment: forced into the grid of media representation and jurisprudence, the war machine is annulled. Yet this annulment will probably never be total, there is always something left over: a remainder of the production of desire, of invention, of an actualization of the possibilities that have been opened up. Following the trauma of Genoa, in the summer of 2002 the PublixTheatreCaravan hence developed increased activity again, especially in the context of the international border camp in Strasbourg. There their war machine consisted of an old English double-decker bus, which again conjoined the two components of technical skill and artistic cunning. The bus was a technical machine, a composite of the old mechanics of the automobile and high-tech equipment inside it, and it was also a concrete localization of the micropolitical social machine of the PublixTheatreCaravan. After their experience in the autonomous squatter milieu, in the transnational anti-racist Noborder network, and in the anti-G8 protests in Genoa, in July 2002 the Caravan machine was ready to be coupled with the social machine of the border camp in Strasbourg. On the open upper deck and around the locations of the bus in the city of Strasbourg (especially the expansive area in front of the train station) new arrivals to the city were greeted, information about the border camp was distributed and parties were enjoyed; yet beneath the splendid surface, in the belly of the bus, state-of-the-art electronic equipment enabled a counter-public media and communication guerrilla praxis …

2000 years earlier, machinic materiality and machination, these two components of the theater machine are found in the predecessors of the Caravan theater and war machine. In ancient warfare, *machina* appears as a technical expression in conjunction with carrying out sieges. From the classical Greek and Hellenist *poliorcetica* to the warfare authors of late antiquity, all kinds of siege machines are listed as *machinae*, especially those for overcoming city walls or for battles at the walls in general. One of the earliest examples for the Latin use of the term *machina* is found in Ennius (early 2nd century BC), and is also evidence for this point of reference: *machina multa minax minitatur maxima muris*, a giant machine that terribly threatens walls. City walls were the focus of attention for these special machines, because for a long time there were no weapons that could breach them; hence combined, complex machines were needed that enabled an approach as secure as possible across moat systems and close to fortification rings with towers, as well as making it possible to conquer or destroy the walls, even if it meant taking them down stone by stone. Yet even here, similarly to the theater machines, it is not only a matter of concrete technical machines penetrating the walls, bringing them down or allowing them to be overcome. Here too, *machina* alternates between the material wall-breaker and the cunning that circumvents the wall or makes it open by itself.

In the 4th century AD, shortly before the period that is generally represented as the collapse of the Roman Empire, although that probably happened much less as a break than is usually presumed, an author who remains anonymous wrote *De rebus bellicis* (DRB), a treatise for the counsel of the emperor in matters of war. In the late 19th century, the text was still called "Denckschrift eines verrückten Projekte-machers" ("Memorandum of a Mad Project-Maker," cf. Seeck), but people started qualifying the text as a "serious work of military engineering" (Mazzarino) and the anonymous author at least as a "brilliant dilettante" (Giardina). The text "about matters of war" is a social reform petition to the emperor in office, proposing reforms of the military in particular against the background of general, one could even say moralizing statements about corruption, extravagance and overtaxation (economic elements of rationalization predominate in this military policy discourse of late antiquity, such as reduction of personnel, reduction of service periods, limited tax exemptions for veterans, operation of war machines by reduced personnel or avoiding the deployment of troops and war machines altogether with more economical forms of occupation).[2]

The main section of the text (chapters 6–19 of 21 altogether) consists of a catalogue of the inventions of war machines with illustrations and brief commentaries. From the text and the use of the terms *inventio* and *inventa* in late antiquity, it is unclear whether the

2. The text of the treatise can be found in the Oxford Text Archive http://ota.ahds.ac.uk/. Cf. also the article on the anonymous author by Seeck in *Paulys Realenzyklopädie I* (1894), 2325; Santo Mazzarino, *Aspetti sociali del quarto secolo: ricerche di storia tardo-romana*, Rome: L'Erma di Bretschneider 1951; Edward A. Thompson, *A Roman Reformer and Inventor*, Oxford: Oxford University Press 1952; Hartwin Brandt, *Zeitkritik in der Spätantike*, Munich: Beck 1988; Andrea Giardina (Ed.), *Introduzione a Anonimo, Le cose della guerra*, Milan: Mondadori 1989.

inventions are all or only partly new inventions, or even inventions by the author—in the Praefatio he points out himself that he has "gathered together everything useful from everywhere." A total of twelve war machines are presented here, which have such intimidating names as Tichodifrus, Clipeocentrus, Currodrepanus or Thoracomachus, but also—the more frequent variation in war machines—with animal names: an entire zoology is to be found in the writings of antiquity on warfare, including "rams," "tortoises," "ram tortoises," "raven's beaks" and "cranes."

In the preface the author boasts of being able to present not only an extremely fast type of ship, by today's standards quite utopian, driven by oxen trotting in a circle on the ship and paddle wheels and a new, easily transportable hose bridge for crossing larger rivers. He also invented a special device for making a horse urge itself on without any command, when breaking through a line or chasing a fugitive. The *currodrepanus clipeatus* (cf. DRB, XIV) is a horse-machine for causing the greatest damage to the enemy without human aid, in other words, even if the rider has been thrown off: *verberibus spontaneis*, "automatically" whipping itself through the masses, this imaginary machine of a battle horse without a rider corresponds to the inverse form of Kafka's rider without a horse. In Kafka's text fragment "The Wish to become an Indian," the rider sheds the spurs and then the reins, finally flying over the ground "already without horse's neck and horse's head." In the invention of the anonymous writer, the horse-machine whips itself on, instead of a becoming-Indian, instead of a machine of becoming-animal, the fantasy of a technical-animal combat apparatus.

However, such imagined predecessors of today's weapons and war technology, which have been largely realized in the development, for instance, of remote-controlled drones, should not mislead us to separate the machines from their concatenations with the invention as cunning. Already by the end of the 1st century AD, in his work on the various forms of stratagems, the Roman commander and senator Frontinus had concentrated—contrary to our anonymous author—on the immaterial. Since in Frontinus' opinion inventions in the area of war devices had already reached their limits, in the third book of his *Strategemata* he turned to tricks and stratagems that could help to avoid or shorten an expensive siege. He listed a total of eleven different stratagems, including enticement to betrayal (bribery seemed to be the most economical procedure for taking over cities), redirecting rivers and poisoning water, terrorizing the besieged, and many more. The most inventive variations of stratagems are in any case those that involve deceiving the besieged. Here Frontinus lists primarily strategies of travesty: Hannibal was said to have taken many cities in Italy by having his men adopt the Roman habitus and sending them ahead—disguised by language and clothing—as spies or the covert avant-garde of the conquering troops. The Arcadians overpowered the troops that were sent to aid the besieged, put on their uniforms and thus took the city in the resultant confusion. The Spartan Aristipp disguised his soldiers as merchants, Epaminondas of Thebes disguised his as women to open the city gates to their armies.[3]

Our anonymous author's war machines have a surplus of materiality that reaches into the immaterial, just as Frontinus' stratagems, on the other hand, rarely get by without materiality. The thesis of the extensive overlapping of material and immaterial components of the war machine crystallizes in an exemplary form, however, in the most prominent myth of the war machine epic. The most famous example of a machine that decides and ends a war through cunning is again a horse, but this time a wooden one. In Virgil's *Aeneid*, three lines before the famous verse, in which the Trojan priest Laocoon expresses his reservations about the gift from the Greeks pretending to depart,

---

3. The judgment of this *locus classicus* on the part of the authors of antiquity oscillates between admiration for cunning behavior and condemnation of insidious deceit, the latter often combined with rhetorically reinforced pejorative allusions to the introduction of groups such as "merchants" and "women" that were understood as excluded from masculine virtue.

quidquid id est, timeo Danaos et dona ferentes, Virgil refers to the Trojan horse as *machina*: *aut haec in nostros fabricata est machina muros* (2,46). Virgil has Laocoon warn that this machine is devised as a trick against the walls of Troy, and this opens up the entire palette of the war machine: from the stratagem of the *fatalis machina* (2,237), through which Odysseus undermines the insurmountable city walls, to the concrete war machine, the *machina belli* (2,151), which does not even have to function as a wall-breaker in this case, but is brought into the city by the Trojans themselves. It is not a coincidence that Odysseus, as a typical machinator, is known not only as *polýtropos* and *polýmetis*, but also by the epithet *polyméchanos*. As the inventor of the technical machine and the psycho-social invention of the Trojan horse, he is literally both multiplying cunning and mastering many machines.

However, Odysseus' poly-mechanics also appear to inhere to the enemies of the Roman Empire, against which the anonymous author of *De rebus bellicis* wrote his treatise. Impelled by his commercial interest, the anonymous author proffered his colorful array of more or less useful war machines to an equally anonymous emperor, who was in need of these inventions to mobilize imaginations against the overflowing fantasies of collapse in the *Imperium Romanum* of late antiquity. The lifestyles of the "barbarian" enemies of the Roman Empire between nomadic wandering and retreat into remote areas, their geographies between snow-covered mountains and the desert proved to be so diverse that very different inventions were required to fight them (DRB, VI). Contrary to the general culturalistic notion of the correlation between Roman civilization and technical progress, of the direct proportionality of Roman culture and military technology on the one hand and the typical topoi of barbarian wildness, destructiveness and ferocity on the other, the anonymous author of *De rebus bellicis* even attributes to the barbarians *ingenii magnitudo*, the mother of all virtues: inventiveness, *rerum inventio*, also in terms of war machines, is by no means alien to them (DRB, Praefatio).

Anonymous's barbarians, which are not specifically identified and thus spark the imagination all the more, come closer to the concept of the war machine in *A Thousand Plateaus* not only in a vague allusion to nomadology, but also and especially in this emphasis on their inventiveness. Nomadic *inventio* starts with the invention of technical machines, but goes far beyond it. Nomads—and with this term Deleuze familiarly and paradoxically means especially those who do not move from where they are—not only invent war machines, they *become* war machines, when they develop inventiveness as a specific mode of action and subjectivation. Here invention means not only the invented device and invented stories, but beyond this the capability of inventing new worlds. Along with and within nomadic existence, fleeing, deserting the state apparatus, the inventiveness of the war machine evolves new forms of sociality, instituent practices and constituent power, the creation and actualization of other, different possible worlds. Rather than seeing the possible as a predetermined image of reality in one *single* possible world, *inventio* implies the differentiation of the possible into *many* different worlds. Counter to the identitary constitution of the one world of state apparatuses, it produces bifurcations into many worlds. Where a single possible world is divided up in the logic of the state apparatuses, the singularities of invention distribute themselves among different possible worlds.

Theater machines, war machines, these are not only the two strongest lines of the differentiation of the *mechané/machina* concept, these two lines also correspond to two of the main components of current social movements and the small revolutionary machines affiliated with them. Contemporary strategies of inventive cunning, of confusion, of asymmetry, of travesty, whose genealogical lines include the polymechanic machinator Odysseus as well as the medieval figure of the jester, the tradition of the Italian politics of *autoriduzione* (the self-organized reduction of rent or the cost of food) in the 1970s, as well as the practice of the communication guerillas of the 1990s, also raise questions about the overlapping between invention and imitation, of (intellectual) property, of the commons and of appropriation. The forms of action used here are usually situated on the boundary between legality and illegality, between play and militant action, purposely blurring this boundary. They are often actualized on the margins and within the framework of social movements, not only constituting, but also sometimes problematizing them and their organisational forms.

For example, a group from Barcelona and Madrid has appeared since 2002 under the name Yomango, carrying out these kinds of practices of appropriation with performative and media strategies. In colloquial Spanish "yo mango" means "I shoplift," and what is shoplifted here is both material and immaterial at the same time: on the one hand, commodities are appropriated in a playful, very concrete manner, but on the other hand also and especially signs. In the name Yomango there is also a formal allusion to the group's practice: the appropriation of the name and the logo of the Spanish transnational textile corporation "Mango" exemplifies their program. Yomango especially likes to liberate products imprisoned by multinational corporations as well as signs that end up in captivity due to rigid copyright policies, imprisoned less by authors than by globally operating corporations. And just as these corporations sell not only their commodities, but increasingly also their brands as lifestyle, Yomango celebrates shoplifting as a lifestyle.

Micropolitical practices such as those of Yomango, the Italian Chainworkers, the *Umsonst* campaigns in Germany, the Hamburg *Superhelden*, all groups that have played a certain role in the spread of the Euromayday parades and the precarity movement, but also the Reclaim the Streets parties of the 1990s or the Clown Army of the anti-G8 summits in Gleneagles and Heiligendamm: they all conjoin the capability of invention as a war machine with performative practice as a theater machine.[4] But even the macropolitics of the "global movement" could be described as a performative movement in the genealogy of theater machines. At the same time, many social movements of the 1990s and 2000s are war machines, because they invent the dream and the reality of deserting the state apparatus. In other words, they also problematize their own closure, structuralization and state-apparatization in Guattari's

---

4. On Yomango see http://www.yomango.net; on the Chainworkers see: http://www.chainworkers.org/; on Umsonst see: Anja Kanngieser, "Gestures of Everyday Resistance," http://eipcp.net/transversal/0307/kanngieser/en; on the Superhelden see: Efthimia Panagiotidis, "The 'Good News' of Precarization," http://eipcp.net/transversal/0307/panagiotidis/en; on Reclaim the Streets and the Clown Army see John Jordan, "Notes Whilst Walking on 'How to Break the Heart of Empire,'" http://eipcp.net/transversal/1007/jordan/en.

have shifted depending on social, geographical and temporal context. Even in the mobilization contexts of the Euromayday movement, an intensive process of exchange has been and is still needed to ensure a reasonably precise differentiation of the concepts around precarity. If the Euromayday parades in many European cities in recent years have renewed the practice of May 1st, in the processes accompanying them these parades are not only to be seen as attempts to politically organize the precarious, but also—both before and beyond this—as communication and information campaigns on issues of precarization, as instruments of collective knowledge production, as militant research into current modes of working and living.

In the course of the present decade an increasingly intense debate has developed throughout all of Europe, ranging beyond the events of the parades to discussions, reading groups, surveys, leftist magazines and other publications, differentiating the core concepts, but without seeking to rigidly define them. Important lines of these debates, which can only be provisionally accumulated here, have suggested deferring an all too enthusiastic identification and overly hasty unification under the umbrella of precarity. Not least of all, the narrow geographical and historical boundaries of the precarization discourse today have been problematized in terms of gender and Eurocentrism. From this perspective, precarity does not appear to be a new phenomenon at all; fordism could be considered as a "Western" exceptional phenomenon of the 20th century, which made precarity invisible within a certain framework and turned it into an exception. Conversely, however, it also seemed appropriate to regard the "new" forms of immaterial, cognitive, affective labor not only as new, as mere components of postfordist capitalism, but rather to investigate their continuities and discontinuities in a more precise and historical examination.

In the discussion of precarious modes of subjectivation outside the realm of victim discourses—especially in the context of the autonomy of migration—it became clear that the extremely different forms of precarization, their differences and hierarchies, should not vanish into a diffuse conglomeration of the precarious. Yet the structure of precarization corresponds to a continuum of separation and division of labor, based on both the production of boundaries and hierarchies and on the constant blurring and dissolving of those boundaries. Against this background, there is little point in making rigid, simple distinctions between subjects of self-determination and those determined by others, constructing two classes of luxury and underprivileged precarized, identifying the former with the "creative class," the "intellos precaires" or the "digital boheme," the latter with migrants or sans-papiers. Just as the complex and diffuse social situation in all these areas produces a link between smooth forms of self-precarization and rigidly repressive forms of labor discipline, new modes of subjectivation are also becoming possible, distributed across the entire continuum, which can be understood as emancipatory. Yet if precarization means not only social subjection and machinic enslavement, but also forms of resistance against authoritarian labor regimes in the genealogy of 1968—those still in existence and also new ones— then there is also little point in speaking of "the pre-carized." Instead of the victimization expressed in the use of the passive form, the term "the precarious" can be used more logically and more in keeping with the ambivalent situation. From this perspective, it also does not make much sense to employ the soci-ological term of "de-precarizing," which seems to imply too much hope in regaining the welfare state. Finally, the palette of the phenomenon of precariza-tion extends far beyond the question of working conditions: from the repeal of guaranteed (and last-ing) employment to the expansion of various forms of so-called "atypical employment" (which has meanwhile become typical even for younger, white, male citizens in central and western Europe) and the extension of working hours into the endless expanses of the terrain formerly called the private sphere, the continuum of precarity reaches all the way to issues of social security and the precarization of life from a bio-political and migration-political perspective, in the extreme case the precarization of residence.[1]

Whereas the conceptualization of precarization, precarity and precariat in movement-related discourses became increasingly intense and dense, the diffusion into other fields was less productive. Debates about a "disassociated precariat" (*abgehängtes Prekariat*) led to a proliferation of terminological confusion in broad sections of the German-

1. On movement-related debates on precarization, see the articles in the issue "precariat" of the multilingual eipcp web journal transversal, http://eipcp.net/transversal/0704, the Spanish and Italian issue of the Mayday newspaper "Milano-Barcelona Euro MayDay 004" published in Barcelona and Milan, the Precarity issue of the Dutch *Greenpepper Magazine* from 2004, the special issue of the British *Mute* magazine with articles on precarity published in the *Mute* issues 28 and 29 (2004/05), http://www.metamute.org/en/Precarious-Reader. Individual articles relevant to the aforementioned lines of discourse include: *Precarias a la deriva*, "Adrift through the Circuits of Feminized Precarious Work," http://eipcp.net/transversal/0704/precarias1/en; kpD, "The Precarization of Cultural Producers and the Missing 'Good Life,'" http://eipcp.net/transversal/0406/kpd/en; Angela Mitropoulos, "Precari-Us?," http://eipcp.net/transversal/0704/mitropoulos/en; Vassilis Tsianos/Dimitris Papadopoulos, "Precarity: A Savage Journey into the Heart of Embodied Capitalism," http://eipcp.net/transversal/1106/tsianospapadopoulos/en; Isabell Lorey, "Governmentality and Self-Precarization," http://eipcp.net/transversal/1106/lorey/en.

speaking mainstream press in fall 2006. A carelessly formulated study had classified the "Germans" (excluding the population living in Germany without voting rights) into nine political types, whereby the "disassociated precariat" was the ninth and last stage of this typology. The ensuing debate left out no platitudes or reactionary resentments, and had an impact not only in the political field, but also far beyond it, reaching into academic and intellectual contexts. The group identified as the precariat was not only fixed to the role of object and victim: the debate around the study went beyond this to construct a new quality of lumpen proletariat and its exclusion from political agency.

Once described by Marx and Engels in the *Communist Manifesto* as "that passively rotting mass thrown off by the lowest layers of the old society," the new, precarious lumpen proletariat was now no longer imagined and described as only passive and pushed into precarity, but rather—particularly insidiously—as self-victimizing agents of their own exclusion. The debate was no longer about exclusionary practices of the majority society, but rather only about the purportedly *felt* exclusion of those affected, about self-exclusion for which the excluded are presumably themselves responsible. The term precariat was intertwined with a neoliberal, self-chosen loser existence. There was no mention here of resistive refusal, but rather of persons who must be subjected to increasing state control, since they obviously do not allow themselves to be neoliberally governed.

This continued discursive exclusion and the denunciatory figure of imputed self-exclusion is an intentional and effective misunderstanding on the part of the normalizing mainstream, a socio-political stratification that the center of society needs to re-constitute itself. At the same time, however, the discursive dynamic surrounding the "disassociated precariat" can also be interpreted as an effect of increasing unrest: as a necessitated defensive that becomes necessary in reaction to the emergence of a new machine, a new monster. The name of the monster is precariat, its historical model and friction surface is the giant proletariat.

As it is used in everyday language, the term "pre-carious" derives from the French *précaire* and means lacking in security or stability, subject to chance or unknown conditions. In Roman law, *precarium*—"secured through entreaty," "revocable," "granted subject to repeal"—was the concession of a right not based on a legal claim. Especially in the contexts of French social sciences, the term has been used increasingly since the early 1980s. Here, however, the broad conventional sense, in which nearly anything could be called precarious, was already constrained to the precarization of labor and the term was disam-biguated as a negative definition, as an identification based on a lack. This line of tradition partly involved a one-sided emphasis on the negative effects of emancipatory currents after 1968 that were directed against authoritarian labor regimes and aimed at self-determined working conditions. The struggles of the 1970s sought to flee from patriarchal order, the factory regime and the subordination of life to the fordist-patriarchal discipline of work. However, the highly ambivalent connection between emancipatory movements and the neoliberal restructuring not only of the working world was only recognized in its full complexity and differentially problematized in the late 1990s. Around the same time, the conceptual limitation of precarity was opened in the direction of bio-politics, social precarization and precarious life. Especially the strands of post-Operaist, feminist and post-structuralist theory insist here on the mutual penetration of work and life, the public and the private sphere, production and reproduction, on a position that does not fall back behind the insights and achievements of the breaks of 1968 and the 1970s or even turns against them, and finally on the development of a concept that uncovers the ambivalence in the precarious.

As I attempt in the following to reconceptualize the term precariat against this background, this attempt is rooted less in an etymological or theoretical genealogy, but rather in the development of the terminology within the movement that has formed around it in recent years.

During the preparations for the anti-G8 summit in Genoa in 2001, a group associated with the media-activist collective Chainworkers in Milan organized a first Mayday Parade. In the afternoon of May 1st not many more than about 500 people took up and developed the non-representationist demonstration forms of the 1990s. Purposely situated not as a confrontation with the traditional May manifestations in the morning, Mayday escaped their celebration of labor with its different problematic connotations. While social democracy and unions throughout Europe still continue to engage in their rituals on May 1st, still propagating "full employment," while some green parties seek, on the other hand, to create a dichotomous counterweight to this with the "day of the jobless" on April 30th, the order of employment and unemployment has long since absconded and transformed itself: into a world, in which not only employment and unemployment become diffused in countless in-between forms, but in which forms and strategies of resistance have been and are still to be invented.

Tying into the radical genealogy of Mayday since the Haymarket Riots in Chicago in 1886 and of the legendary US American union of the Wobblies, the International Workers of the World, from the start the new tradition of May 1st has had an international orientation, seeking to problematize precarization as a transnational phenomenon. The early development of precarization in Italy explains initial attempts to organize and mobilize the "generation of the precarious" specifically in Milan, of which the alarm signal and battle cry "Mayday!" soon sounded beyond the Italian borders. The slogan on posters, flyers and banners, however, was not "Stop Précarité" [Stop *Precarity*], as it was first developed by part-time workers at French McDonalds restaurants in the course of a campaign in winter 2000. Instead, the slogan was "Stop al precariato" [Stop the *Precariat*]. This somewhat confusing formulation is connected with the various meanings of the term precariat in different languages today, but also with differing allusions to the historical concepts of the proletariat. In Italian, *salariato* (cf. also the French *salariat*) roughly means the legally defined status of wage labor against a legal and social-institutional background. From *this* perspective, *precariato* is the other side of this statute, the one *without* regulations or rights. This is what is to be fought against, and the spread of it needs to be stopped. In everyday Italian, the word *precariato* means particularly the area of employment where no fixed rules are to be found in terms of employment situation, wages and the working day.

A number of things changed in 2002. Not only has the influx of parade participants grown to an astonishing extent, especially in the year after 9/11 and Genoa, which has often simply been described as a traumatic break in the anti-globalization movement, but the central slogan has been virtually turned around: there was no longer any talk of stopping the precariat, but quite the opposite—"Mayday. Il primo maggio del precariato sociale" [the first May of the social precariat]. A two-fold turn occurred here: with the reference to the social, struggle and reflection were expanded from focussing on work to the precarization of sociality, of life, and most of all, instead of an evil to be forestalled, precariat became a self-designation. The "precariato sociale" developed into a common designation for a multi-layered and multifaceted mass that does not describe itself as a victim, but rather as a social movement. This semantic transition was completed a year later, when the slogan on posters, flyers and banners was: "Il precariato si ribella" [The Precariat Rebels].

By 2003 the spread of the movement was already evident in the actualization of the transnational potency of Mayday: the parade was announced as "la parade del precariato Europeo," not only because precarization was recognized as a transnational problem, but also because more collectives and groups from other European countries participated in organizing the parade in Milan. Yet the increase in participation was not limited to the level of quantity and transnationality, but also extended to forms of action. Among others, the bicycle activists from

Critical Mass joined in, quickly and effectively when it was a matter of occupying and reappropriating the street. As "apripista della mayday parade," the swarm of the critical bicycle mass opened up the stage of the city.

As a consequence of transnationalization, in 2004 a transformation of the Euromayday Parade occurred with a first simultaneous organization in Milan and Barcelona. On the evening of May 1st, 2004, some ten thousand demonstrators marched from the central square of the university through the city to the beach of Barceloneta: sans-papiers and migrants, autonomous activists, political activists from left-wing and radical leftist unions and parties, art activists, precarious and cognitive workers of all kinds, who were just working on naming themselves precari@s. Like a moving and accelerated version of the practices of Reclaim the Streets, a stream of dancing, chanting and painting people flowed through the inner city of Barcelona. The streets that the demonstrators passed through were transformed into painted zones. Under the protection of the demo, the city was dipped into an ocean of signs: political slogans, posters, stickers, references to web sites, labeled pedestrian crossings, contextualizing wall painting commented on here and there by performative actions. The spread of creativity, the diffusion of the artistic into the society of cognitive capitalism, thus struck back once again: as the logos and displays of corporate capitalism that uniformly distinguish inner cities are indebted to the creativity of a multitude of cognitive workers, the creativity exercised in these jobs now spread out as an opponent over these logos and displays of the urban zone of consumerism—over the display windows, city lights, rolling boards and LED screens as well as the walls of the buildings and the streets. A mixture of adbusting, cultural jamming and contemporary political propaganda reigned as a generalization of the street art of sprayers and taggers: an abstract machine concatenating invention and performativity, war machine and theater machine, the assemblage of signs and the assemblage of bodies. And over all of this was a slogan expressing the continuum between insecurity and fear in precarious living conditions and the threat of the terrifying monster precariat in all its contradictoriness: *La inseguridad vencerá*, insecurity will prevail …

Barcelona 2004 gave a crucial impetus to the transnationalization of Euromayday. Italian and Spanish activists produced the web site http://www.euromayday.org and the Mayday newspaper that was published in two versions, in Italian and Castilian/Catalan. After 2004 international Mayday meetings took place in various cities of Europe, usually around the edges of leftist conferences and social forums. The "Middlesex Declaration of the European Precariat" in fall 2004 heralded the explosive spread of Euromayday, and following the meeting in Berlin in January 2005, which was propagated as the "International Meeting of the Precariat," the parade spread increasingly throughout Europe. In 2006 and 2007 there were Mayday parades in over twenty cities, although with somewhat different political orientations and varying quantities of participants.

The machinic practice of inventing and concatenating bodies and signs, the theatricality and the flight from representation generated different qualities and quantities of reappropriating the city and discursive space in the various local contexts: whereas hundreds of thousands of people have taken to the streets in Milan in recent years, in the Slovenian city of Maribor there is only a small group of creative activists who have had to deal with all the more severe legal repression. In Berlin (where there has been a Mayday Parade since 2006), a mixture of more conventional modes of demonstrations (performances by left-wing bands before the parade, encouraging speeches from the first wagon of the parade) and new forms of action have been tried out, whereas the Hamburg Parade since 2005 has done without stages and speakers' platforms. The specific experience of Vienna, where the first parade was also organized in 2005, was the long route of the parade through the city, waltzing through the city for four hours. Here too, there were no stages, but instead an endeavor to thwart the familiar hierarchies of podium and audience, speakers and listeners, and the logic of prominence and big names. The parade flowed from one hot spot of precarization to the next, pausing at each of these specific places. There, jingles were played, briefly describing the quality of precarization in the respective context (from sex work to deportation practices to labor market policies). Granted, the technology did not always work, many could not hear the jingles, the connection to the respective sites could sometimes only be imagined, yet nevertheless an attempt was developed to conjoin a practice of non-representationist expression with a concrete strategy to situate precarization.

In Vienna (and not only there), the activists insisted for a long time on the necessity of understanding the Mayday movement as a process, as an ongoing struggle. From this perspective, the Euromayday machine has two temporalities, not only that of the event, the parade and the actions around it, but also the long duration of instituent practice, in which the context of the abstract machine as a movement problematizing precarization becomes evident. However, the idea of continuously spreading the discourses and actions over the year could not be fully adapted to the resources of desire and time. The micro-actions and discursive events as well as regular communication through the mailing lists are usually focused on the first four months of the year, becoming increasingly intensified until May 1st. The information and discussion events held prior to May 1st, the militant research and self-questioning, the multifaceted text and discourse production multiplies and condenses knowledge about precarization every year, and at least in some parts of Europe a small, but increasingly dense network of problematizing the precarization of work and life has emerged.

6

ABSTRACT MACHINES

[…] an abstract machine of mutation, which operates by decoding and deterritorialization. It is what draws the lines of flight: it steers the quantum flows, assures the connection-creation of flows, and emits new quanta. It itself is in a state of flight, and erects war machines on its lines.
— Gilles Deleuze/Félix Guattari, *A Thousand Plateaus*

Vitruvius, Roman architect, himself a builder and theorist of war machines under Caesar and Augustus, wrote in the first century BC about the machine: *machina est continens e materia coniunctio maximas ad onerum motus habens virtutes*, the machine is a coherent concatenation of material components and has the greatest virtues in moving heavy things. Two definitive conceptual components of the machine are already found here, composition and movement, which later prevail in the lexica and specialized books of the 18th century in the definition of the term machine. Christian Wolff, master of mechanical philosophy, defines the conceptual components of the machine in his *German Metaphysics* from 1719 as follows: "A machine is a compound work, whose movements are grounded in the type of composition." *Compositio* and *motus* are the two decisive and mutually interrelated components of the machine, for Wolff both at the micro level of the body and at the macro level of the world as machine, which is in turn composed of machines. Let us overlook, for the moment, the problematic aspect of the totalization of the world that occurs here and concentrate on the quality of the two components and their relationship.

Raising the question of the mode of composition and its connection to movement means to me to focus on the specific *social* composition and recomposition of *social* movements. Contrary to every empirical definition of "class situations," I want to describe social composition explicitly not as a state, but as a movement. In this way, I am ultimately aiming for a specific form of composition that flees, avoids and betrays the concepts not only of the state apparatus, but also of the community. Initially this means taking up a motif here again that is found in a continuity of the terms for the composition: the machine—and this is the conventional modern notion, also Wolff's—as *compositio*, as a (cunning, artificial) composition of parts that do not necessarily belong together, but at the same time also the machine according to Vitruvius's definition from antiquity as *continens e materia coniunctio*, in other words as *continuum* and *concatenation*, as an assemblage in which the parts are imagined as neither a priori isolated from one another, nor robbed of their singularity in a unit. What both notions suggest in our context is a conceptualization as a vessel, which is not striated towards the inside, which is open to the outside and designed for communication. The communication of the machines and machine components, of singularities, of monads thus does not appear guaranteed by God as with Leibniz or by any other universal, but rather as a concatenation of singularities, as a profoundly polyphonous, even a-harmonious composition without a composer.

A social composition of this kind sets itself against the state apparatus as a striating container, as well as against concepts of the community as a natural body and unit closing itself off to the outside through identity and totality. These two major patterns of classification are what the machine as a social movement separates itself from: from the state and from the community.

The search is thus for a formless form of the political concatenation of singularities, which are not structuralized in the form of the state apparatus and its components of stratifying and dividing space, but at the same time one that does not close itself off in the large, all-amalgamating inclusion of the community. The machine sets itself against the "artificial" state form and the striating of its interior, hence also against the absolutist metaphor of the "state machine," *and* against the "natural" form of the community—and this apparent dualism of "artificial" and "natural" can only be named here in quotation marks, standing for two different modes of forming and classifying: the mode of the "artificial" striation and the mode of the "natural" enclosure and totalization of an interior posited as absolute. This second figure constructed by naturalization and incorporation applies not only to the historical cases of early Christian communities [*Urgemeinschaft*] or fascist people's communities [*Volksgemeinschaft*], and even the critique of contemporary right-wing communitarianism is insufficient here. It is to be feared that behind even the high-minded discourses of the affronted (Jean-Luc Nancy: *La communauté affrontée*), unavowable (Maurice Blanchot: *La communauté inavouable*), inoperative (Jean-Luc Nancy: *La communauté désoeuvrée*), or coming (Giorgio Agamben: *La comunità che viene*) community there lies a process of identification, a desire for collective identity without cracks, without rupture and without an outside. In these readings of community, it is possible to distinguish new forms of machinic enslavement beyond the old problems of communitarianisms and in addition to the social subjection of the subjects by the state apparatus. Here, in service to the communal unity, control and self-control interweave as modes of subjectivation and form a new *dispositif.*

Counter to this interlocking of government and self-government, of social subjection and machinic enslavement, and in order to deepen the anti-state and anti-communitarian quality of the machinic concatenation, I want to take a slight detour to the early works of Jacques Tati. In film criticism Tati's works are frequently misunderstood as civilization-critical complaints against the demands of modernity. Especially Tati's first feature film *Le jour de fête* has been (falsely) interpreted this way, due to its idyllic framework (and its ludicrous synchronizations). In the sequence of *L'ecole des facteurs* (1947) and *La jour de fête* (1949), in which almost all the scenes from the "School for Postmen" were included, however, it is evident that Tati's first feature film can be seen as anything but a hymn to a return to village life in the country. The sketch series *L'ecole des facteurs*, barely fifteen minutes long, is more than a preliminary study; the small film clearly shows the point that Tati is aiming for. As a pure parody of the military disciplining of postmen and the striation and rationalization not only of their working day, but also of every detail of movement in the fordist framework of labor, the "School for Postmen" shines with mini-attractions that thwart this regime. These extremely physical tricks especially on bicycles, which are typical for Tati, follow one another in quick succession in *L'ecole des facteurs*; in *Le jour de fête* they are slightly hidden by the many details of village life and the seemingly contemplative frame of the plot.

The first feature film that Tati wrote and directed himself begins and ends as a bourgeois idyll, but it develops its strengths as a burlesque that seems from today's perspective less anti-modern/anti-fordist, but more proto-postfordist. During a fair the carnies show a newsreel about the most recent methods for modernizing the postal service in the United States. Sorting machines, air mail and post helicopters provide the optimum realization of the Taylorist motto "time is money." With images of daring motorcycle stunts mixed in, the American mailmen prove themselves pioneers of modernity. The country postman François, played by Jacques Tati himself, sees these images and is captivated by the new spirit of the times. From this point on, his motto is "*rapidité*—speed!" and he becomes obsessed with modernizing his simple job. *Le jour de fête* becomes quite prophetic in the scenes in which François, inspired by the abstract machine of the newsreel film, breaks through the peacefulness of his village community and makes the division of labor of the postal state apparatus implode. On the same evening Tati makes his protagonist (in other words himself), intoxicated by the celebration, by alcohol and by the incipient effect of the images that showed the possibilities of a modern postal system, melt into a machine in incredible tricks with his bicycle. The next day he mutates into

"Monsieur Postman," while the motto "*rapidité*!" becomes an anticipation of postfordist modes of production. François rides faster and faster with increasing virtuosity, emulating the figures of the American motorcycle stunts with his bicycle, riding it through fire, confusing the order of traffic, and leads the field in a spurt in a bicycle race. Then his bicycle rolls by itself, escaping from the fordist forced community and waits, casually leaning against the wall of a pub, for its owner chasing after it. It is a motif that recalls the *Third Policeman*, where bicycles also like to run away, if they are not tied up, bound or locked up …

Finally Monsieur Postman packs up all the necessary utensils in the post office to become post himself. He flees not only the context of the village community and the rigid order of the post, but his frenzied flight from the community and the state apparatus is, at the same time, an invention: the invention of a new office in motion. Taking the constant acceleration of movement and work to an extreme, the bicycle acrobat attaches himself to an open truck, spreads out letters, stamps, seals on its open plank in the back and opens his mobile bicycle post office. As a self-entrepreneur he becomes the post himself—similar, in a way, to the monomaniac production machine of Tati, battling against the extreme division of labor in the genre of film. Towards the end, François, intoxicated with speed, lands in the river with his bicycle and is saved by the bent old woman meandering through the whole film with her goat as an allegory of rural life. She brings Francois to safety in farm work, yet the idyllic conclusion is deceptive: in the final shot a small boy wearing a postman uniform runs after the traveling fair wagon, the *rapidité* virus spreads throughout the world. Thirty years later, all of Europe is infected.

Monsieur Postman lives a possible form of resistance: no return to community aids against the new forms of atomizing individualization, as the dichotomy of individual and community is altogether irrelevant in this *dispositif*. In contrast, Jacques Tati proposes an offensive strategy of accelerated singularization. Yet what are the machines, in which these singularities could become concatenated instead of becoming stuck in the identitary containers of the community and striated by the state apparatuses? What is the nature of the new, unbounded tie that is actualized not as a homogenizing coherence, but rather as a multiple concatenation, "tied together by the lack of a tie"?

Karl Marx approaches this question in his early text on the *Poverty of Philosophy* by describing the social composition as a militant process of constituting: "Economic conditions had first transformed the mass of the people of the country into workers. The domination of capital has created for this mass a common situation, common interests. This mass is thus already a class against capital, but not yet for itself. In the struggle, of which we have noted only a few phases, this mass becomes united, and constitutes itself as a class for itself." It is not a coincidence that Marx wrote these clear words about the class emerging in struggles, which were later to be instrumentalized as fuel for legitimizing the party as the all-controlling state apparatus, in his response to Proudhon's *Philosophy of Poverty*. The question of composition and organization remained a matter of contention between communist and anarchist camps over the course of centuries. For its part, the Marxist-Leninist literature quickly reduced the struggle and the process of constituting a "class for itself" to the opposition of the "class in itself" and the "class for itself." A larger social group, parts of which live under the same or similar social and economic conditions, describes in this reading a "class in itself." However, the empirical objectification of this group regards individuals as being unconscious of the common tie.

With Marx there are two figures of subalternity that do not even correspond to the unconscious status of the "class in itself," and these figures have several things in common with the current precariat, both with the construct of the "disassociated precariat" and with a possible precarious potency. The classical example for the state of separation in its extreme form, which cannot even be regarded as a "class in itself," thus also for the impossibility of intervening action and joint struggle, is that of the French small-holding peasants. Marx wrote in 1852 in the "Eighteenth Brumaire of Louis Bonaparte": "The small-holding peasants form an enormous mass whose members live in similar conditions but without entering into manifold relations with each other. Their mode of production isolates them from one another instead of bringing them into mutual intercourse. The isolation is furthered by France's poor means of communication and the poverty of the peasants."

The small holding is the paradigm of isolation. In the situation of spatial separation, the peasants achieve an exchange with nature, but not an "intercourse with society." The concept of intercourse [*Verkehr*], which Marx also shared with his individual-anarchist adversary at the time, Max Stirner, here means something more than a common empirical class foundation. The arbitrary addition of similar units, in Marx's image the many potatoes in a potato sack, does not result in a union, a political organization. On the contrary, under the radical populist government of the "second Napoleon," Louis Bonaparte, the small-holding peasants are condemned to isolation and separation, to the impossibility of intercourse and—which Marx explicitly emphasizes—to the incapability of their own representation. Their mode of existence and production, which is based on a radical division of space and the isolation of the bodies, makes every practice of exchange, of intercourse, impossible. From the perspective of the specific Marxist-Leninist jargon, it is precisely the small-holding peasants' absence of relations and communication, their extreme isolation, that lacks the precondition for becoming a "class for itself." The small-holding peasants are not even a "class in itself," cannot become conscious of their common situation and develop general strategies going beyond local confrontations. They lack the potentiality of the "class in itself," the potentiality of people whose economic conditions identify them as a class, but who have not yet realized what they have in common, not yet founded an organization, because of their living conditions.

Yet Marx also has another figure of the unorganizable outside: the lumpen proletariat. Here it seems that everywhere that Marx's concept of the proletariat has been fixed in an identitarian logic, its outside, the lumpen proletariat, and its sharp separateness from all that organizes, through a positivist and moralizing description has also been fixed. The problematic aspects of this kind of fixation can be seen on the one hand in the notions of identitarian logic in scientific Marxism, which identify and classify a clearly distinct group of people as the proletariat, and on the other hand in the canonized figure of the dictatorship of the proletariat. From this perspective the lumpen proletariat becomes a combination of the last remains of a pre-industrial era and a contemporary, but transient appearance of the industrialized city: "Alongside decayed roués with dubious means of subsistence and of dubious origin, alongside ruined and adventurous offshoots of the bourgeoisie, were vagabonds, discharged soldiers, discharged jail-birds, escaped galley slaves, swindlers, mountebanks, lazzaroni, pickpockets, tricksters, gamblers, *maquereaux* [pimps], brothel keepers, porters, literati, organ grinders, ragpickers, knife grinders, tinkers, beggars — in short, the whole indefinite, disintegrated mass, thrown hither and thither, which the French call *la bohème* [...]." Whereas the small-holding peasants were compelled to remain in their situation of a non-class due to their empirical situation, in the "Eighteenth Brumaire" Marx moralizes the lumpen proletariat as the "scum, offal, refuse of all classes." And the constant, the connection and presumed representation of both sectors of the population construed as the absolute outside, which cannot or will not organize themselves, paradoxically proves to be the head of the state. Louis Bonaparte is and constitutes himself as the head of the lumpen proletariat and the small-holding peasants.

Somewhat surprisingly, in addition to the afore-mentioned categories of work-shy counter-revolutionary subjects (as the historical analogon of the "disassociated precariat") in the "Class Struggles in France," Marx also counts the financial aristocracy (perhaps as the analogon of the "digital boheme") as belonging to the lumpen proletariat: "The finance aristocracy, in its mode of acquisition as well as in its pleasures, is nothing but the *rebirth of the lumpen proletariat on the heights of bourgeois society*." In other words, with this heterogenization of the lumpen proletariat there is already an image of the outside permeating society, which cannot be equated with a "lower class." Marx's complaint of the unproductivity of this diffuse lumpen proletariat can be seen as an early form of the construction of the disassociated precariat, as an imputation of intentional self-exclusion, self-elimination and self-marginalization; and certainly the combination of the small-holding peasants excluded from intercourse and the lumpen proletariat unwilling to organize does not initially shed much light on the question of social recomposition. Here, however, one could also recognize the possible conditions of the precariat as an offensive figure of concatenation, as an expansive successor to a diffuse lumpen proletariat on the basis of the general allotment of work and life.

In the classical Marxist-Leninist schema, the sleeping giant proletariat, unlike the adventurous lumpen and the isolated slaves of the small holdings, only needs to first awaken, to be awakened through class consciousness and party. In other words, it correlates with the situation of the "class in itself" and only has to come to itself, become "for itself," through the right form of organization. The proletarians as members of the lowest class, which only served the Roman state of antiquity by providing progeny (*proles*), from the Marxist perspective the wage-laborer without ownership of the means of production, implies homogeneity in many respects. Even just this figure of the wage-laborer represents a normalized dominant, the proletarian "class for itself" all the more so, which emerges through the specific forms of organization of unions and mass political parties and which, most of all, can only take up the struggle against the ruling class as a *unified* class.

Even though the allusion of the term to the proletariat suggests regarding today's precariat as movement and organization of the dispersed precarious people, in terms of the dispersion of the actors it is more analogous to the small-holding peasants, in terms of the broad social situation more analogous to the figure of the lumpen proletariat. Unlike the image of the sleeping giant of the proletariat, which must be awakened through class consciousness and a political party, the precariat is a monster that knows no sleep. There is no teleological movement here from sleeping to class consciousness; there is neither the empiricism of the class itself nor the political invocation of a class for itself, but rather a constant becoming, questioning, struggling. The precariat cannot stand for an empirically determined problem nor for a future model of salvation. Nor is it in any way simply the other pole of precarity, somehow analogous to the "class for itself" in its relationship to the "class in itself." The figure of the precarious indicates dispersion, fragility and multitude. The precariat does not represent a unified, homogeneous or even ontological formation, but is instead distributed and dispersed among many hot spots, not only because of weakness or incapacity, but also as a discontinuity of geography and production, as distribution in space. Whatever form the concatenation of the precariat assumes, whatever forms of (self-) organization it develops, the term itself indicates that in its modes of cooperation it does not fall back into uniformity and structuralization. If the precariat *is* anything at all, then it is itself precarious.

To grasp the machinic quality of this potentiality and precarity of the precarious, let us open up a final etymological view into the broad space of Indo-European languages. Here the Greek *mechané* and the Latin *machina* prove to belong to the etymological line of the hypothetical Indo-European root *magh-*, which is probably related to the old Indian *maghá* and the Iranian *magu-*, referring to the semantic field of "power, force, capacity." In addition to echoes in various Slavic languages, *magh-* is also the root for the German word *Macht* ("power") through the Gothic and Old High German *mag* for "*mag, kann*" (cf. also the Anglo-Saxon *maegen*) and the Gothic *mahts*.

If we want to make use of this etymological line for our questions about the machinic mode of social composition and concatenation, then instead of under-standing this power as a synonym for domination, we take it initially—following Foucault—as a relation of forces. In this sense the machine is not the means of a powerful subject, which thus accomplishes its metabolic exchange with nature, but rather a differential relationship, an assemblage that provides impulses for specific modes of subjectivation. Most of all, however, following Spinoza, power is to be understood here *before* any stratification, appropriation and instrumentalization as potency, capability and possibility.

This potency, this capability is the power of abstract machines. The terminological constellation of the powerful-possible-machinic and of abstraction first of all permeates potency and actualization. In this respect, abstraction does not refer to dissociation, misappropriation, detachment, or distancing from the "real." The separation of the social from the technical machine or the general from the particular is specifically not what distinguishes the abstractness of abstract machines. Instead of actualizing abstraction as detachment, as separation, I understand abstract machines as transversal concatenations that cross through multiple fields of immanence, enabling and multiplying the connections in this field of immanence. The way that abstract machines correlate with capability and possibility, does not imply that they were first separated from "reality" in order to then "grow together" with this real in the condensation of concretion. Abstract machines are neither universals nor ideals, they are virtually real machines of possibility. They do not exist before and beyond, but rather on this side of the separation of assemblages of signs and assemblages of bodies, forms of expression and forms of content, discursive and non-discursive *dispositifs*, what is sayable and what is visible. They exist on this side of the separation, yet they do not exacerbate the opposition of bodies and signs, but rather enable them to flow together.

The "transcendental" abstract machine, which remains isolated at the level of the outline, which does not succeed in conjoining with concrete concatenations, is only a special case. Lethal machines like the legislative-executive machine in Kafka's *Penal Colony* or the love machine in Jarry's *Supermale*, no matter how complex they may be, are "dead" machines because they lack socio-political concatenations: the machine that carves the judgment into the delinquent in the *Penal Colony*, pronouncing the judgment god-like directly in the body, establishes an unmediated relationship between bodies and signs, but after the death of the former commander, whose law it had obeyed, it has no link to social machines. Its case is similar to the love machine, which falls in love with the "supermale," then turns around and kills the lover: the machine, actually built to propel the "supermale" to enhanced love performances, takes on a lethally high voltage and breaks off every concrete concatenation. The "supermale" dies like the officer in the *Penal Colony* in the machine, not as its component, one of its gears, but as its raw material. And yet the union of the mechanized human and humanizing technical machine persists at the stage of a one-dimensional exchange relationship in "transcendental" abstraction. For machines, which like the judgment pronouncing-executing machine in the *Penal Colony* and the loving-killing machine in *Supermale* cannot extend and expand in a montage, the logical end is self-*de*montage, self-destruction.

So much for the special case of the "dead," "transcendental" abstract machine. But how could a "living" abstract machine be imagined, what are its quality and intensity, what are its components? The power and abstraction of the abstract machine are evident in three components, into which a deep ambivalence is inscribed: diffusity, virtuosity, monstrosity. 1. The diffusity of the abstract machine means being dispersed among the most diverse production locations, modes of production and social strata. 2. The virtuosity of the abstract machine means its quality as abstract knowledge, cognitive and affective labor and general intellect. 3. The monstrosity of the abstract machine means its disposition as a formless form.

In his "modern novel" *The Supermale* (*Le Surmâle*, 1902), Alfred Jarry created a paradoxical anti-hero, who is actually a perfectly conventional, almost exaggeratedly normal human being. Physical exercise does not particularly agree with the "supermale" Marcueil, he is not fit enough for it. The "man whose strength is boundless" gets sea sick on the train and is afraid of accidents. And yet in the interplay and confrontation with machines Marcueil develops "superhuman" machinic powers, becomes himself an abstract machine. Even though the novel is constructed as a mad utopia and situated in the future (1920), the diffusity, virtuosity and monstrosity of the "supermale" is an immanent one. In the "ten thousand mile race," the mad race between a Rapid Express and a five- or six-man bicycle team, the race between machine and man is to be decided. "Lying horizontally on the five-man tandem—the 1920 standard model for racing: no handlebars, fifteen-millimeter tires, covering a stretch of seventy-five meters thirty-eight with each rotation of the pedal—, our faces lower than the saddle and protected by masks to keep us free from wind and dust, our ten legs on the right and left each linked together by an aluminum rod." Not enough that the cyclists represent a complete merging with their machine, they are also doped with a special food, the "perpetual motion food," the marketing of which is actually the occasion for the ten-thousand-mile race.

In the test of strength between the mechanical steam machine and the doped bio-machine there is no evident advantage for some time. Over long stretches the train and the human super-racing machine are on a par, even if one of the cyclists expires from exhaustion or as an effect of the doping in between: "You can sleep well on a machine, you can just as well die on a machine." At first the others strain themselves to pull the corpse along ("this dead body sat there buckled on, girded on, under seal and officially certified on its saddle"), then it comes to the "sprint of the dead Jacob" ("a sprint that no living person could even imagine"), and the racing bicycle takes the lead again. More and more indications appear, however, that there is a third, unofficial competitor involved: a "shadow," a hunchback that increasingly sets out to pass both competitors. "Yet at a speed like ours, neither anything living nor anything mechanical would have been capable of following us." Exactly: the thesis of the book is that there is an AND, living *and* mechanical, that is not at all to be found only in the progressive merging of man and technical machine. The "supermale" crosses the path of the other two teams as the "half-wit cyclist"; he jolts, stumbles and pedals in the empty air, riding a bicycle without a chain. His chain did not break, "he rode a chainless machine!" The Rapid Express burns up its wagons, the racing cyclists slash their tires to avoid taking off, and yet they have no chance against the half-wit cyclist supermale riding in zigzag lines. Faster than light, he passes up the locomotive and the racing machine.

1. When Marx, in the "Eighteenth Brumaire," names the poor means of communication of the French alongside poverty as a particular obstacle to the organizing of the small-holding peasants, the most numerous class in France, he hits an important point, the variability of which could also represent a qualitative turnaround for the question of how to link the

small holders of today. In a sense, the dispersion and isolation of the French small-holding peasants is actually repeated under current postfordist conditions, and the refusal to organize of the lumpen proletariat "thrown hither and thither" is repeated as well. Diffusity, abstraction in the sense of dispersion and precarization lead in this respect primarily to competition, lack of solidarity, and opportunism. Yet as the political and economic circumstances at the time of the industrial revolution were somewhat different from those of today in advanced postfordist capitalism, the question of a new potentiality of the concatenation of singularities and struggles arises anew. Communication among the small-holding peasants in the 19th century must be primarily imagined as direct communication. The dispersion of the locations and modes of production was necessarily accompanied by isolation, in contrast to concentration in the factory. For the seemingly analogous phenomena of a new dispersion in the transformation from the dominant fordist paradigm of the factory to the postfordist affective and cognitive paradigm, however, a different situation applies. This paradigm is veritably *based* on cooperation, intercourse, exchange, all aspects that virtually function as the imperative of postfordist production.

Instead of the clearly negative connotation of dispersion as obstructing all social intercourse, the present conditions offer an ambivalent situation, which manifests both a lack of direct communication *and* the potentiality of new forms of communication in the dispersion. Thus, to the modes of existence in abstraction, in diffusity, there also inheres the potential in itself to generate concatenations of singularities instead of identitary and communitary forms of societization. Whereas the French small-holding peasants were not only dispersed, but also in servitude under the old communal forms of family and village, today new forms of concatenation are to be invented that make use of the diffusity of singularities to desert from machinic enslavement and social subjection: concatenations of chain-less machines connected by the lack of any ties.

Undoubtedly, means of communication today are mostly accessible to increasingly wider circles. Even the extreme geopolitical inequalities in this respect are in upheaval today. At the same time, it is clear that these changed conditions are not necessarily to be equated with an emancipatory use of media progress inherent to the media. Machinic enslavement, conducting modes of subjectivation beyond social subjection, is the governmental shadow-side of the potentiality even of advanced means of communication. The dependency on machines is multiplied through the continual attachment to the machines, the constant mode of being attached to machines. The high art of machinic enslavement interlocks a permanent online life with the imperative of life-long learning and the irresolvable merging of business deals and affects. The streams of desire of the ubiquitous attachments generate new forms of dependency, which make the material penetration of the technical machine into the human body appear as a secondary horror scenario. And yet, the desiring machines are not simply tools of machinic enslavement; the minor advantages of the resistive use of new abstract and diffuse machines in dispersion are by no means always already over-coded.

2. Beyond the technological and communication-technical conditions, the crucial material of abstract machines is knowledge production and cognitive work. If the diffusity in cooperation, intercourse and exchange is the structuring imperative of postfordist production, the virtuosity of abstract knowledge is its central raw material. Marx describes the machine of the industrial revolution in the Fragment on Machines as having a soul of its own, being self-moving and, most of all, being itself a virtuoso. It takes this virtuosity from the workers, whose virtuosic handling of their instruments, their tools, once animated and moved these, but whose labor on and in the machine merges into an activity that is "reduced to a mere abstraction," "determined and regulated on all sides by the movement of the machinery." In this relationship there is a sharp separation between virtuosity and abstraction: the machine appears as a virtuoso, the activity of the worker as abstract. Here I would not

call for a reversal and return to the earlier relationship between workers and means of labor, but rather question the separation of virtuosity and abstraction. This separation blurs under the present conditions of cognitive capitalism, in which virtuosity increasingly correlates with abstraction.[1]

To examine this assertion, we can return again to the concept introduced by Marx in passing, the concept of the *general intellect*, also the explicit starting point for the Italian (Post-) Operaists for their ideas on the struggles of mass intellectuality and immaterial labor. In *The Grammar of the Multitude*, Paolo Virno picks up directly from Marx's machine fragment and the concept of the general intellect. Whereas in the era of industrialization social knowledge was supposed to be completely absorbed in the technical machines, this becomes unthinkable in the postfordist context: "We should consider the dimension where the general intellect, instead of being incarnated (or rather, *cast in iron*) into the system of machines, exists as attribute of living labor." Virno emphasizes that constellations of

1. On the question of virtuosity after and beyond Marx, cf. Hannah Arendt, *Between Past and Future*: Viking, 1968; Paolo Virno, *A Grammar of the Multitude*, Semiotext(e), 2004, especially 52ff.; Isabell Lorey, "VirtuosInnen der Freiheit. Zur Implosion von politischer Virtuosität und produktiver Arbeit," in: *Grundrisse* 23, http://www.grundrisse.net/grundrisse23/isabell_lorey.htm.

concepts develop specifically within contemporary labor processes, which themselves function as productive machines, "without having to adopt the form of a mechanical body or of an electronic valve," and thinks the machinic beyond being cast in iron especially in the fields of abstract knowledge and language.

In Virno's theses, Marxist and poststructuralist machine theory, Marx and Guattari finally overlap. Because of the logic of economic development and the development of modes of production itself, it is necessary to understand the machine not as a mere structure that striates the workers, socially subjects them and encloses social knowledge within itself. Going beyond the Marxian notion of knowledge absorbed in the fixed capital of the machine, Virno thus posits his thesis of the social quality of the intellect: in postfordism, the raw material and means of production of living labor is the capacity for thinking, learning, communicating, imagining and inventing, which is expressed through language. The general intellect no longer presents itself only in the knowledge contained and enclosed in the system of technical machines, but rather in the immeasurable and boundless cooperation of cognitive affective workers.

Taking over the Marxian concept of the intellect with an emphasis on *general* thus indicates that intellect is not to be understood as the exclusive competency of an individual, but rather as a transversal, machinic-social quality, as abstract knowledge in the sense of the concept of abstraction earlier alluded to. The generalization that resonates in the concepts abstract and *general* is not, even though it would seem to suggest itself, to be understood in the sense of a totalization or universalization, but rather as the tendency of a potentiality that is open to all sides, shared by all. Virtuosity enters into social labor as a workless activity, its score is the general intellect. The "trans-individual" aspect of the general intellect refers not only to the totality of all knowledge accumulated by the human species, to the commonality of a shared capacity assumed to be antecedent, but most of all to the action of living labor coordinated between cognitive workers, their communicative interaction, abstraction and self-reflection, their cooperation. However, the objection should be raised in contradiction to Virno that no anthropological constants of any kind are needed to imagine singular-abstract intellectuality, not even a "pre-individual" quality of language and reason. Specifically this separation of the sayable from the visible, the general from the individual, the abstraction from virtuosity is, in fact, what is thwarted by abstract machines.

3. In the idiosyncratic back-and-forth between the worlds, between the various zones of strict immanence, as it occurs in Flann O'Brien's *Third Policeman*, there is an uncanny underground region, an eternity machine, which the two policemen always

have to hold in a certain balance, so that their "measurements" do not shoot up into the "danger zone." At the entrance to eternity there is an elevator descending at an incredibly fast speed. Eternity itself proves to be a combination of long passageways and gigantic halls that all look exactly the same.

The eternity machine is called that because time does not pass in its interior. Yet not only time stands still, but also space—eternity has no size at all, "because there is no difference anywhere in it, and we have no conception of the extent of its unchanging coequality." Accordingly, there are also things in this immeasurable space that have no known dimensions, that evade every description. Even their shape cannot be grasped by the eye. They have the special feature of being featureless, the special form of formlessness.

Abstract machines are things like this, which have themselves no form, are formless, amorphous, unformed. Yet their unformed-ness is not to be understood here as a lack, but rather as the ambivalent precondition for the emergence of fear as well as for the invention of new, terrifying forms of concatenation. At one pole of current modes of existence in cognitive capitalism there is formlessness as the trigger for the overflowing and interlocking of fear and anxiety—whereby this blurring assemblage cannot be reduced to a psychological or anthropological category or a desperate fight to return to fordist wage labor conditions. The uncertainty of working conditions, irregular ways of living and the omnipresence of precarization allow anxiety to become diffused in all social situations as a no longer purely mental problem. At the other pole there is formlessness as the potentiality of the development of a terrifying monstrosity: new dangerous classes, non-conforming masses, micropolitical precarious monsters. Here abstract machines are to be understood as anti-identitarian non-form and potentiality of forming, which trigger clear forms of expression and content in concrete concatenations. The power and capacity of abstract machines are found in the monstrous attack on the striated/striating form of state apparatuses and on the amalgamating enclosure within the community.

Once again: the diffusity, virtuosity and monstrosity of abstract machines are to be seen as basically ambivalent. Like all machines, abstract machines are productive components of cognitive capitalism; they can be coopted as soon as they are made or imagined, as soon as they are invented. However, ambivalence also implies here that in every thinking, every experience of immanence minor advantages of a not yet coopted machinic difference emerge. These advantages are probably the source of the great charm that is sometimes also about bicycles, such as on May 19th 2007, when the *ladyride* moved through Vienna: as a queer appropriation of the mass bicycle rides of the

Critical Mass and, at the same time, of the feminist genealogy of the bicycle in the first women's movement. Under the motto "Won't you bike my ladyride?," a group of *ladyfest* activists of all genders rolled from station to station. These stations involved the political situating of the city and its stolen, silenced and looted stories, from the trans-les-bi-gay victims of National Socialism through the history of sex work to migrant labor struggles. A swarm of thieves on bicycles reappropriating the street and the city in a queer feminist city tour on wheels. There was not only sight-seeing along the route, though, but also collective traffic calming and spontaneous street blockades. "Honk, if you love us!" was a motto then, or: "Wer ist der Verkehr? Wir sind der Verkehr!"[2]

It is precisely in this that the quality of the machine beyond humanist, mechanistic and cybernetic interpretations consists: in the insistence of a dissonant power, a monstrous potency and enjoyment, in the ambiguous re-invention of *Verkehr* as a non-conforming concatenation of differences, singularities and multitudes in an a-harmonious composition without a composer.

---

2. "Who is the traffic/intercourse? We are the traffic/intercourse!" Here we find a threefold bifurcation of the German word "Verkehr": 1. the concrete traffic of the cars, bicycles and persons in the city space, 2. the queer appropriation of the sexual connotations of "Geschlechts-Verkehr," 3. the social intercourse and exchange in Marx's and Stirner's sense.

ACKNOWLEDGMENTS

This book itself is a small machine, and since my name is attached to it "purely out of habit," there is also no reason not to name those who have aided, challenged and inspired me and much more: the ongoing collaboration and discussions with Isabell Lorey, Stefan Nowotny, Marcelo Expósito and Aileen Derieg, the friendly criticism of the machine concept in my book *Art and Revolution* by Alice Pechriggl and Karl Reitter, advice and suggestions from Martin "pyrx" Birkner, Jens Kastner, Tom Waibel, Marty Huber, Birgit Mennel, Klaus Neundlinger and Vassilis Tsianos, the militant energy of the Vienna Euromayday plenum reliably swelling towards every May 1st, the proliferating cooperation with the publishing houses Turia + Kant (Vienna), Traficantes de Suenos (Madrid) and Semiotext(e) (New York / Los Angeles), the friendly neighboring zones with the journal *Grundrisse*, in which two preliminary works for this book were published following extensive discussions with the editors, and finally the network of our institute, the eipcp, expanding throughout Europe and beyond.

Printed in the United States
by Baker & Taylor Publisher Services